Embracing Mind

EMBRACING MIND

BY
KOBUN CHINO OTOGAWA

EDITED BY
JUDY COSGROVE AND JOSEPH HALL

Jikoji Zen Center
2016

Printed in the United States of America

First Printing, 2016
ISBN 978-0-9985374-2-9

Jikoji Zen Center
12100 Skyline Blvd Los Gatos
CA 95033

www.jikoji.org

© 2015 Jikoji Zen Center

CALLIGRAPHY

by Gerow Reece

CHAPTER PHOTOS

1. Kobun Chino Otogawa

2. Sojun Mel Weitsman, Ananda Dalenberg, Shunryu Suzuki, Kobun Chino Otogawa, Dainin Katagiri San Francisco Zen Center

3. Kobun Chino Otogawa Colorado

4. Kobun Chino Otogawa Puregg (House of Silence), Austria

CONTENTS

FORWARD

Angie Boissevain

As a weekend guest at Tassajara Zen Mt. Center in its very first years, a monk told me about Haiku Zendo in Los Altos, not far from where I lived, and about Kobun Chino, the Zen Master there, and recommended I look him up. A young mother of three boys, painfully shy, but already inspired by the zazen practice I learned at Tassajara, I timidly found my way to little Haiku Zendo, on a suburban street in Los Altos. Once there, after the first long sitting, I glanced up, met Kobun's eyes, and was scared and awed to realize this practice was what I had been searching for for as long as I could remember.

After a few months, I began attending his Monday morning teachings, and there began to help Mary Kate Spencer write down Kobun's slow slow speech as he discussed basic Zen sutras. This writing practice developed into typing all the Monday morning material, and then into also transcribing the taped talks Kobun gave during our five sesshins a year, becoming a many-years-long labor of love for the Dharma, and for my teacher.

When I met him he was in his early 30's and had only been in the United States a few years. A small man, he sat before us in meetings speaking extremely softly and slowly, his English awkward and original, as he gestured with gentle hands. The Dharma he expressed seemed to emerge in slow spirals, and we learned to listen with our hearts and bellies, and had to abandon linear thinking as he spoke. Some complained because he didn't make "sense;" some relished this new way to speak, pointing to what can't be said.

Kobun was a poet, a brilliant calligrapher, and a landscape painter. But with demands for his teaching, he had little time for art. Not only had he accepted Suzuki Roshi's assignment of Haiku Zendo, after helping him set up Tassajara, but Roshi, on his deathbed, asked Kobun to help San Francisco Zen Center Sangha complete their training after he passed away. Kobun also taught classes at Stanford University, and, as well as Wednesday nights and Thursday morning meetings with students, sat five sesshins with us every year.

The forms he taught were the basic ones established by Dogen Zenji 900 years ago. Eating rituals, service, sesshin schedules were strict and traditional. Other more complex ceremonies were simplified. A Full Moon Ceremony was held around a bonfire, Shuso Ceremony in a living room. Ordinations were sometimes very precisely traditional, and sometimes, depending on the student, hardly noticeable.

In those suburban years, he encouraged families to form among us, and formed one himself with his American wife, Harriet, and, in a few years, two kids, Taido and Yoshiko. Living around the corner from Haiku Zendo, he easily could walk there, and sesshins were only 3 miles away on a ranch in the country, so he could slip from sesshin to go home and tend to his family, as many of his students could also do as well. Retreats were always open to such comings and goings to accommodate needs of the sangha.

After he moved to New Mexico to found Hokoji temple in Taos in the '80s, we seldom saw him, but the California sangha gave full attention to developing two permanent practice places, Kannon-do temple in Mountain View and Jikoji, a retreat center in the Santa Cruz mountains, to which he came and went as he widened his life and practice to serve many others, in New Mexico, and in Europe, where he founded new temples with Vanja Palmers.

He died in 2002 in Engelberg, Switzerland.

Angie Boissevain

The more you sense the rareness and value of your own life, the more you realize that how you use it, how you manifest it, is all your responsibility. We face such a big task, so naturally we sit down for a while.

~Kobun Chino Otogawa

INTRODUCTION

Shinbō Joseph Hall

In 1967 a ship arrived in San Francisco. Aboard was a Zen Priest, carrying with him a large bronze bell and a wooden mukugio sent as gifts to honor the establishment of the first Zen monastery in America. The instruments would later burn in a fire at Tassajara Monastery and the young, shy priest would never return to live in Japan.

His birth had been a fortunate one. The Otogawas were a respected family of priests and in 1938, Kobun was born in the family temple at Kamo, a small town in the Nigata province located in Northwestern Japan. He was the youngest of six children in a prosperous and stable country. Quickly, circumstances changed. World War II began and lasted the bulk of Kobun's early childhood. Kobun's father died when he was eight, leaving behind a family foraging for food in a devastated Japan. Sometimes the family ate pumpkins, sometimes they ate pumpkin stems.

Even at an early age, Kobun was a skilled and intuitive calligrapher and a bright student. He found a mentor in Hozan Koei Chino Roshi and began serious Zen training, ordaining at the age of twelve. At fourteen he was adopted by Chino, who had no heirs, and began the training to prepare him to inherit the abbacy at Kotaiji. Together, the two walked from household to household performing ceremonies.

By high school, the draw toward a simpler practice led Kobun to sit with Kodo Sawaki, who was advocating a revitalization of zazen practice and a turning away from ceremonies and chanting. Kodo would have a powerful influence on Kobun and an irony began to develop: Throughout his life as a priest, Kobun would stand out for his exquisite ability to perform ceremonies and he would be well remembered for his predisposition not to do them.

Wandering the divide between these two antithetical teachers, Kobun mirrored the teachings of each with an embodied sense of place wherever he was. With Chino, he ministered to his people, performing flawless ceremonies, guiding them through the rites of passage in their lives. At Antaiji, he wholeheartedly rejected any adornment to the simple practice of seated meditation and sat in stoic silence with Kodo. To Kobun, both his teachers were exactly right.

Kobun had found a home in paradox. Inhabiting this dynamism, Kobun's mind unequivocally embraced the world exactly as he found it.

Graduating from Komazawa University in Tokyo and then earning a masters degree at Kyoto University, Kobun did his monastic training at Eiheiji and received dharma transmission from Koei Chino Roshi in Kamo in 1962. He continued to practice calligraphy and trained in kyudo, formal archery, with Sensei Kanjuro Shibata. By 30, Kobun was a classically educated Zen priest and was offered a post at Eiheiji, one of the two head temples of Soto Zen, where he trained Eiheiji's monks in the ceremonial forms.

Kobun was now fully immersed in a bastion of Japanese tradition, but not even Eijeiji was impervious to the changes of the late 1960s.

The traditional tool of monastic discipline was the kyosaku, a wooden sword-like stick that was used to wake-up the young monks whenever their concentration began to wander. Kobun took exception to the idea of corporal punishment and asked for and received permission to set aside the kyosaku in the training of novices. Kobun further broke with tradition on the question of gaijin.

The Japanese word for foreigner is "gaijin", a phrase meaning "barbarian" and, after centuries of isolation, the word, gaijin had no better definition then the Americans who were arriving at Eiheiji in the 1960s. Although he didn't know it yet, Kobun was about to become part of a social revolution in America. The call that brought him there was not one of politics, but a stance of simple compassion.

In San Francisco, another Japanese priest who had been sent to run the local Zen temple had quietly started to work with a group of Americans seeking to expand their consciousness. The little sitting group grew quickly into the San Francisco Zen Center and Shunryu Suzuki somehow managed to get a few of these counterculture Gaijin into Eiheiji for training. Watching these radicals enter the temple gates, Kobun saw not barbarians, but human beings...

"I did a small kindness to the American students who were utterly stuck in the monastery (Eijeiji). Suzuki Roshi had sent them, and they were having enormous difficulty. It's beyond imagination. Literally, aliens had landed in the monastery! One [Phillip Wilson] was a regular member of Stanford's football team. Huge.

Muscles. When he stands, he really stands out, literally. Small Japanese people. Everyone is short. His body, about from here up, stuck out. He walked like a dinosaur! Another person [Graham Petchey] was an English gentleman, taller than him, like a crane flying with those wild geese. They were very obvious, and their knees hurt so much, and they wanted to eat chocolate, and they wanted to go to the dentist, and everything! So I ended up looking after them and protecting them from hardship.

In Eiheiji monastery there is no freedom allowed. They could speak no Japanese. I only could speak a little bit of English, but I could listen to them very carefully to hear what the actual problem was. Everyone thought they were lying, that they wanted to go to the hospital in order to take a break from practice. I ended up taking them to a doctor to check on their knees, and to a good dentist to fix their teeth. I didn't know that was all reported to Suzuki Roshi or that he came to look at me in the Zendo one day."

-Kobun Chino Otogawa

Kobun Chino Otogawa & Shunryu Suzuki at Tassajara

In 1967, the San Francisco Zen Center purchased property and established a monastery at Tassajara Hot Springs. Suzuki needed someone to train these novice monks in formal monastic practice and he sent an invitation to Kobun at Eiheiji. Kobun made the traditional request to his teacher three times and permission was denied. Despite this, when the ship left Japan to carry the formal gifts from Eijeiji to the first Zen monastery in the United States, Kobun was aboard.

Arriving in San Francisco, Kobun joined Suzuki and Dainin Katagiri, who would later establish the Minneapolis Zen Center. Kobun taught the Americans the subtleties of Zen practice but, quietly, the more he worked to establish an institution, the further he seemed to drift away from it.

Kobun stayed at Tassara until 1969 when the forms had taken root. Finally, the day came to return to Japan and complete his training with Chino, who was growing increasingly impatient with his erstwhile protege. Suzuki, on the other hand, saw something different in Kobun and while he accepted his decision

At Tassajara: Dainin Katagiri, Taizan Maezumi, Bill Kwong, Shunryu Suzuki, Sojun Mel Weitsman, Richard Baker, Kobun Chino (Far Right)

to return to Japan, Suzuki said, "You can go, but you are the kind of person who should live in *this* country."

Kobun returned intending to live in Japan. It turned out to be a shortlived homecoming. Travel had become entrenched in Kobun's way. Six months later, Haiku Zendo in Los Altos, where Suzuki had originally intended Kobun to teach, brought him to America for a second time and he was installed as Resident Teacher in 1970.

His style was informal. He preferred to be called by his first name, Kobun, not Chino or Otogawa, and never Roshi, He encouraged his students to think of him as friend - not master. His unpredictable and subtle style resonated with the times as he emphasized life-in-the-world, encouraged his students to marry and have children and he exhorted them to live the Dharma like guerrillas.

Like Eiheiji, Haiku Zendo soon discovered that this teacher of the still mind school also had an immutable evanescence. In short, Kobun could be anywhere in any given moment but rarely where one might expect him to be. Sitting groups affiliated with Kobun began to appear in the Silicon Valley and Santa Cruz, he taught Buddhism at Stanford and a few other local colleges and he began to establish temples and practice centers. He was integral to the formation of the Santa Cruz Zen Center and founded Hokoji in New Mexico, Jikoji Zen Center in the Santa Cruz Mountains and Felsentor Zen Center in Switzerland. Kobun was at once shy and gregarious and was captivated by spiritual practice wherever he found it. He was close friends with Trungpa Rinpoche and was instrumental in the establishment of Naropa University where he held the Wisdom Chair. When Steve Jobs started Next computer while on hiatus from Apple, Kobun Chino Otogawa was listed as it's Spiritual Director. Through his connections with people, the Zen of Kobun Chino was beginning to ripple through American culture.

While he founded four temples in America and Europe and a growing number of sitting groups and practice centers continue to sprout up in his lineage, Kobun ventured out from the San Francisco Zen Center with the clear idea that his vision of Zen in

America was not a large institution. The spoke and hub model of a quiescent teacher surrounded by a cadre of students felt stifling to him. Like many of the Japanese teachers who brought their religion to the new world, his formal education had made it clear that Buddhism always evolved with each culture it encountered. In the fertile soil of America, Kobun set out quietly to plant the seeds from a Japanese bonsai and allowed each of them to grow to their full height amongst the redwoods. No two trees seemed to grow alike.

Some students, like Michael Newhall, sat with Kobun inspired by his intricate knowledge of Buddhism and the way with which he flowed through a world of objects and circumstance. Kobun deflected this devotion and turned it into quest, leaving Newhall to follow this voice in his heart across America and into Japan, through academia, art galleries and temples. Newhall became an artist and professor of Buddhism, teaching at Naropa and the Art Institute of Chicago until eventually traveling to Japan to refine the forms of his teacher within himself before settling in as the Guiding Teacher of Jikoji. Without words, Kobun's instruction seemed clear: "If you want to know me, you will have to examine the world."

Kobun demonstrating the art of Calligraphy at Naropa University,

And in the world, the mark of Kobun was indistinguishable from the work of the people he encountered. Naropa has cultivated a new generation of American Buddhists. Vanja Palmers, Kobun's Dharma heir, has nurtured a new generation of Kobun's students in America and Europe. Steve Jobs reimagined a way to merge Zen and technology to create forms that we carry in our pockets ingraining both the aesthetic of Zen and the opportunity to creatively engage it in dialogue within our culture and our daily lives.

Kobun's life ended suddenly. In 2002, his daughter, Maya, fell into a pond in Switzerland. Kobun dove in after her but was unable to save her and in the water and they left this world together.

~

Defining Kobun is no easy task. Each person you interview seems to have encountered exactly the Zen teacher they were looking for. In the eyes of his students, Kobun sometimes seems to epitomize Wild Zen, in another moment a vision of cultivated civility is painted in the mind, in yet another turn he is simply a soft-spoken teacher sitting atop a mountain or a street corner. Often, his rejection of dogmatic form seems to define him as an anarchist. But like a Jazz musician, what is easily missed is that Kobun first mastered the classics before he ever thought of composing on the fly.

The most striking thing about this Zen teacher was the intimate grace with which he moved through this world, which seems to come alive every time his students talk about him. For Tim Burkett, Guiding Teacher of the Minneapolis Zen Center, that moment comes in watching a group of people tread their way across a creek and then seeing the agile steps of Kobun gliding along the same stones, unhindered through the obstacles and possibilities of his path wherever it wound.

Zen is said to be a practice of embodiment. The texts and words we study are likened to a raft which carries us across a river but which then becomes a burden when we arrive on the other shore. Left to translate what made Kobun singular among the

generation of Japanese teachers who brought Zen into flower on American soil, what is said over and over is that this person seemed to

embody the form of an enlightened being. It was something you saw the moment you met him, that somehow you had never seen a person move like that, seemingly aware of every detail filling the moment and the world he inhabited. What Kobun had was grace.

It was a grace large enough to contain a great irony. Kobun could create ceremony gloriously, whether at Eiheiji or standing in a field of grass under a full moon. Classically educated, he taught Buddhism at Naropa and Stanford, established liturgy at Tassajara, and was a master of calligraphy and kyudo, ceremonial archery. And yet, with an arsenal of skills to teach, Kobun set formalism aside and insisted on teaching only what arose from the soil of a country in which he was a stranger.

If there is a single quality that defines the teaching of Kobun Chino Otogawa, it seems to be this - the Buddha has no body but ours. Again and again, he turned his students away from a conceptual view of Zen and his clearest instruction to us is to look for Buddha within our hearts. While enlightenment is the simple nature of all things, the place we hear its voice most intimately, the only language we can understand, emanates from deep within ourselves. Kobun's trust in this voice and his delight in hearing it from his students was indefatigable. As a lineage gathered around his teaching, Kobun was more interested in listening.

Shinbō Joseph Hall
Jikoji Zen Center
December 2016

EDITOR'S NOTES

Judy Cosgrove
As far as I am aware, sesshin talks given during the first couple of years with Haiku Zendo students were not recorded, or preserved. The basis of the present text is transcribed and edited recordings of Kobun's sesshin talks between 1974 and 1993. After 1980 these were held at Jikoji Zen Temple, although some of the material also presented here comes from Monday Morning Class, held during the early 70's in various homes. Angie Boissevain, who has dedicated much of her life to preserving Kobun's teaching, transcribed most of the talks. Without her continuing effort in typing out the words from audio tapes, tapes which were difficult to decipher, there would be no record of his words. He never wrote them down in English, and never spoke from notes, making frequent references to Buddhist history and stories from memory.

Quick checks on spelling and references to Buddhist teachings involved many visits to numerous books and websites. Sanskrit or Pali terms were put in italics when first introduced, and romanized Japanese terms in quotation marks. It seemed to make sense to eliminate the italics and quotation marks if the terms were repeated many times. On the other hand, some terms, such as *Vipassana*, and *Shamatha*, which were not commonly used in Kobun's teaching, were more appropriately kept in italics.

This text is divided into four sections, each representing a sesshin named for an aspect of Buddha's life and teaching. Rohatsu sesshin is in memory of Buddha's enlightenment, Denko-e is in honor of the teaching relationship, Tanjo-e celebrates Buddha's birth, and Nehan-e, the Buddha's final Nirvana. Subjects were organized within these broad themes, although Kobun, himself, often varied his lectures according to what struck him as appropriate for whatever was happening in his and students' minds. Here, it made sense to focus on zazen practice more intensely in the text chosen for Rohatsu, and Buddha's teachings in the form of Precepts, for Nehan-e.

Judy Cosgrove

TANJO-E SESSHIN

ASSEMBLY ON BUDDHA'S BIRTH

Chapter 1

Something Brought You Here

".... Along with this questioning, there is hope, and the endless desire to live, no matter what. It is just like the centuries of battles between nations, revenge after revenge. It's happening in your own self."

The Inner Battle of You

After a long journey, returning here to join sesshin gives me great pleasure, merging with your way-seeking energy. Something deep within your mind brought you here, more complicated than "way-seeking mind." It may be a bundle of questions, an urgent need to be filled, an urgent thing to express, in each person. Usually we reach toward a place to practice with some confusion, finally hearing some hint of possibility, who to see, where to go. Most of you started that way, with a sense of your own confusion, your inner dilemma. It's important to remember this from time to time. Is this a familiar feeling for you? Was there a need to find a teacher, some guidance in your practice? It may seem that we came to sit together almost as an accident, but it was the innumerable efforts of your own direct ancestors, their seeking of the way, which is your own inner dynamic, which brought you to the practice.

We have been sitting week-long sesshins on this occasion of Buddha's birth for twenty-one years, since I came to this country. Buddhist tradition flowered out of Buddha's supreme enlightenment, throughout its long history, but we have very little proof of what his actual experience was. We know as little about the historical Buddha as we know about ourselves. This may be the closest way to approach him, since, as far as we know, sitting originated from his experience.

How to see the life experience of Shakyamuni Buddha is up to you, each of you, according to your own understanding. Today, the first day of sesshin, you have been experiencing, very deep within you, centuries of battle. You may question your own nature, whether it is essentially good, whether or not you are helpless, unable to change. Along with this questioning, there is hope, and the endless desire to live, no matter what. It is just like the centuries of battles between nations, revenge after revenge. It's happening in your own self. The battles out there look external, but since you cannot ignore them, they cannot be separate from you. They become the inner battle of you.

Avidya

Basic ignorance, avidya, is unavoidable, even when we are learning various things through our sense organs. Vidya means clarity and its contents. Avidya is absence of vidya. Even if you are a learned person, still you cannot avoid the basic avidya, "no wisdom." When you live alone, the world and universe are perfect to you, almost everything is clear. Yet this knowing of your own world, without knowing what another's world looks like, is like a shellfish looking at it's shell. You think this is the universe when it is just the internal field of the shell. There may be nothing wrong with it, but you still have curiosity about how other people experience their lives. Even when we discuss cultural differences, different religions, different academic fields, still, we are very much blind about others' worlds. We hope everybody experiences things similarly, but come to know that everybody experiences things slightly differently.

Even when we are walking, driving, still this avidya is with us. It means we do not know exactly what we are, what our essence of life is. When you meet a new person, you say, "Tell me about yourself," and they say, "My name is so-and-so, my personal history is so-and-so." You can also ask the same questions about yourself. We have been taught various objective truths, but they are actually just suppositions: "Maybe I am a man," "Maybe I am a woman," "Maybe this, in the United States, is the best way of life." Even when our comparative, conceptual knowledge piles up and is analyzed, there is still "maybe." This attempt to understand, become conscious of the self, is objective self, which doesn't exist. Alas! The life we live is not necessarily what we have studied or discussed. This conceptual, knowledge-based self is nothing but a game of created self-consciousness, an image of ignorance, so to speak. Life has to be freed and lived, instead of being known. Knowing never satisfies, although knowing is one of our major intellectual functions. It's as if you say, "Oh, I got it," and then go to sleep.

Buddha Nature

All of us have, deep inside, basic sanity, an intuitive understanding of how to find the safest spot from which one can see in every direction. This intuition is quite foggy, for many reasons, including various pollutions, and so much information which almost destroys your sense of purity and clear vision. Still, you all know the basic purity of life that continuously lets you survive and feel alright. You have found that sitting is a great opportunity to let this basic sense of continuous new life sustain its purest state. Although sitting is sometimes boring, with no excitement happening, I know you all know about true nature. We call it "Buddha nature," which makes you feel truly and meaningfully alive and not dead. Trusting your whole presence as Buddha nature is the first step to walk in the Buddha's way. Before you take that step, even if you have precise knowledge about the world, that is just a blink of knowledge. This knowledge doesn't help decide which way to step forward, who to meet, what to do, in this world.

Silence

In early Buddhism, silence, holy silence, was kept by monks, nuns, laymen, and laywomen, all who joined the assembly. There were many things you were not encouraged to do, and things you were not to talk about, including war. Silence was encouraged. These days, we come from daily life to sesshins, and talking is difficult to avoid. One starts to talk, the other has to respond. If you are spoken to by somebody, you don't feel good if you keep silence. It ends up with everybody talking. Your concentration space goes somewhere else. Talking is a fine thing, but during sesshin, especially, you do not talk to each other. It is not a rule, it is something very important which each of us has to observe and concentrate on. We are just beginning sesshin, so I have to say something about it. It doesn't mean you go away somewhere all alone during break. When you see somebody walk around in "shashu," walking mudra, with eyes on the ground, unless it is very important, you don't utter words. Especially around the kitchen, keep it as quiet a space as possible. Talking disturbs the cook, who is working hard, and you may end up with burned rice or something. Three places, especially, are silent: Zendo, bathroom, and kitchen.

Holy silence is the space where your psyche can be totally free, without hindrance. It is like clean air with no dust. Mind is captured by matter but when matter is not there, the mind recovers its nature, which is time and space itself. It is not just the concept of space, but actual space, actual time, without ignorance.

In this kind of gathering, you don't need to talk. In the end, you know everybody without talking. But you do silent conversation, always. Usually, conversation goes horizontally, to another, but when it comes back, it's vertical, going deep inside you. This is the deep nature of silent conversation. At some point the need for ordinary conversation stops, and no talk is needed. Keeping silence is not a rule, of course, it is just the nature of this kind of effort.

Tapas

At first Buddha studied with two meditation teachers, but was not satisfied with their teaching, so he turned to very hard tapas practicers. Their ascetic practices included stopping breathing, stopping eating. Day and night they sat, without lying down. For many months they did not take a bath in the river. They were just dust and skin. Kids came around and teased these practicers with sticks and little pebbles but they didn't move or respond.

The basic idea of *tapas* was dualistic, the separation of body and mind. It was believed that the spirit dwells in a transient body, so the purpose was to release the spirit from this limited, dense, sometimes filthy and chaotic, body. It was the visible vs. the invisible, restraint vs. freedom. After six years of vigorous practice of tapas Buddha went into the river to bathe. Afterward, he could only crawl to the shade of the tree. Offered food, he ate and began to recover his strength. While sitting there, Mara came to tempt him, whispering in his ear, "You look so exhausted. Your chance of achieving enlightenment is only one out of a hundred. You'd better get up and take care of your body." But he continued to sit. In the end, what Buddha found was that body and mind are inseparable, an inseparable entity. They differ from each other, but without one, the other cannot exist. So he quit observing his existence as a dualism, and turned to diligent, earnest, continuous practice, guiding him to the purpose of life.

Such a man seems very familiar, because we, each of us, have that kind of seeking of the way. Your mind may feel exhausted and torn apart, and unable to recover its original purity. You may have feelings like, "I'm no good," or "My broken heart can never be mended." Is that truly so? It gives us just a moment's comfort to hear that every existence has Buddha nature. Yet, the next moment we may be in a very alone state, hard, competitive, with a racing kind of consciousness. The enlightened Buddha's world is not so familiar, but a hellish place is much more familiar. This is our experience. This is the field of our belief. In spite of living in this suffering world I continue to believe that nothing can stain the purity of each existence. That is my understanding. That is how I feel when I say all things have Buddha nature, equally. This means that, in an absolute sense, no one can harm your life.

Chapter 2

Why Buddha Left Home

"This refers to the awakening nature of our life, or the alertness required in the insecurity of constant, daily change."

Why Buddha Left Home

Sometimes the question stays in my mind of why Buddha Shakyamuni left home. Yesterday we talked about something urgent within us which drives us to practice. You might say it is a call of Buddha nature in everyday life. This refers to the awakening nature of our life, or the alertness required in the insecurity of constant, daily change. This alertness is something to do with maintaining balance in each of our lives, among all existences, within and without.

Transiency

One realization leading toward way-mind is a feeling about change, rapid change, bringing a realization of the transient nature of all things, which drives you to practice. You want to find some kind of subtle, unchanging self. This realization of transiency may come with experiencing your direct family members passing away, friends suddenly going without saying goodbye to you. You never see them again. So you think that some day, any day, it could happen to you. Perhaps, before they left, you thought you had some clarity about yourself and the world. Maybe, before you lost them, you had experienced a certain perfection in your life. But with this awareness of the transiency of life you are driven to seek for what is called enlightenment. You want to recover that feeling of perfection.

Bodhicitta

The drive to seek enlightenment is like a fire which, once lit, you cannot stop. In Sanskrit it is called bodhicitta. And when it burns, your surroundings, the immediate people around you, are affected by how you live. If you are too different from all other people, you will find yourself in the monastery. And if you spend some length of time in the monastery, you may sort of flow out of the monastery. It is like a persimmon tree whose fruit drops after ripening, and you discover you are among people, all alone. What do you do with your life, then? Some people keep a monk's life, a single life. Some live as an ordinary person, except that you keep a monk's mind within, but your wife is next to you, children are with you. But still something is burning within you. So it is something to do with continuous burning and feeding of way mind. Unless you feed it, you can't satisfy yourself.

This way mind includes an almost painful recognition of independence. Not necessarily aloneness, rather, it is being born alone, and passing on all alone, that kind of realization. You do depend on others, others depend on you, you know that, but it is in essential independence and essential caring, coming from an independent person toward another independent person. In this sense each one of us is absolutely equal. You can say that before the Absolute all are equal, but there are not two, but one person, who is you.

Buddha's Birth

It is my habit, when springtime comes, that I feel very energized and happy about Buddha's birthday. According to an old manuscript, Buddha's actual birth was around May on our calendar. His mother was thirty-five years old and his father was about the same age. Buddha's father was the head of a noble family of the Shakya clan, which governed the small country called Shakya in about the mid-sixth century before Christ, so it was rather long ago. At the present time, the place where Buddha was born, about the middle of the Fifth Century, B.C., is in southern

Nepal. The Shakya clan, which was in the warrior class, was fighting over land in the area, and was later conquered while Buddha was still alive. Society was going through a lot of change at that time. This uncertainty of life woke up people, and they started to look for their own path to peace. Consciousness of individuality was one of the new ways of thinking, and today we are descendants of that beginning attitude, continuing to question how to take care of this individual life. As we seek out examples, guiding teachings, we discover a jewel-like light in the dark, forgotten past.

Siddartha Gautama was about thirty-five years of age when he was enlightened under the Bodhi tree, about four hundred years before Christ was born. I always go back to relive what kind of mind he had, what sensations he was experiencing. After many years of a gorgeous life, with a wife and child, he decided to follow those who left home to seek the way. According to various biographies, his background was a mixture of the Aryan race and native people who lived there before Aryans came to northwest India. We can hardly picture what kind of body he had, what kind of eyes and voice he had.

The Buddha's birth was rather sudden. It was unusual for an Indian family of their class to have a child so late, and they were joyful. But, alas, Buddha's mother passed away from complications from his birth. Her younger sister, Mahapajapati, raised Buddha. In his biography he speaks of how well he was taken care of by her. When he was growing up, he wore sheer, fine silk from head to toe. Many household people were always running around everywhere, and there was always music. When he went out a big parasol was always lifted up. As usual, a fortune teller was called, and the sage, Ashita, spoke, "If this boy stays in the Shakya family, he will become a great ruler. If he doesn't stay in the house, he will become 'one who rolls the chakra, the wheel of teaching.'" The parents were glad, but a little worried that someday this boy would go away, so they prepared especially favorable things around him as he grew up The biography says he married three ladies, and his only son, Rahula, was born to him and Yasodhara.

We don't know exactly what happened, but Buddha left the castle to join the Sramana, and eventually began doing tapas. He practiced this way for six years, finally approaching death. One of the practices was holding his breath for a long, long time between inhalation and exhalation. It causes long minutes of no breathing. We cannot do this more than 10 seconds. Also, he allowed himself no eating, just a couple of grains a day, or a little bit of cow dung, and no bathing. He finally looked like he was eighty years old, with no flesh, just bone and wet paper hanging from the bone.

When I read biographies of various kinds about Buddha's life, it is clear he was a very unusual person, a genius, you might say. When I was growing up in a temple, I was curious to know what kind of person he was. After all of my effort, still he is unknown to me, full of mystery.

Buddha and Others' Suffering

Sramana was a term for those who were not of the Brahman caste, but, like Brahmans, left home to follow a spiritual path. Maybe Buddha joined them because of the shock he felt after seeing people in the streets. Do you remember the story? He was taken to various places and he saw villagers lying on their death beds. Usually he was prohibited from looking at them, but one day he saw a person who was lying down along the street. It was not just one, but many, and since he was very sensitive, he identified with them. He was young, but he couldn't stand the thought of becoming aged. One time he saw a baby being born. On such occasions, most people when they see a poor person in this kind of situation, don't feel that this is happening to them, telling themselves it's others' business. Today, on the TV, we are kind of exposed to those experiences everywhere, and many times we are actually deeply moved by them. Even if we, ourselves, are healthy, we can sense something serious is going on.

Recently, when I traveled through New Delhi, Calcutta, and other places in India, I felt Buddha's life very close. It wasn't just imagination. I felt a slim, very slim, hand pulling me, holding my sleeve, walking with me. The person was still moving, but legs were gone. It's hard to believe such a body is still alive. One day, in the midst of a busy street in Calcutta, we saw a baby being born. It was a beggar's family who had just had their third baby, a slippery, shiny, big head and tiny body. Still had the enormous cord attached. They were so happy to have this baby. I have never seen such a glorious face as that father. People are passing by and looking at it, and passing by. We went back to the hotel, but my heart was pounding so hard, I went back and looked at it again. Have you been in India? You've got to see it. It's a very shocking country. Shakes you up. In my pocket there wasn't so much money, but I wanted to give at least half of it. That country made me think so much. Every night I stared at the ceiling and thought, "What a country!"

I went on traveling, but in each country, even in Japan, I started to think very similarly, how absurd life is. I am really glad to return here and sit with you.

Chapter 3
Mara

"...this kind of sitting practice is like the root of a tree, or foundation of a building, very invisible...life, itself, is in pain."

All Beings are Nothing but Pain.

When I returned from town today, I felt a very wonderful sensation. When I stepped into the Zendo you were sitting so deep. It was the sitting before dinner. I think you know what I saw, the feeling of a person who is approaching the peak of a mountain with great confidence, step by step. At the same time, one is very exhausted and doesn't know what it feels like to be on top of the mountain. The third day of sitting usually feels like that. It is hard, but the inner battle of mind adjusting your physical condition to sitting is almost ending. You feel like you are becoming a bird or something, after sitting such long three days, but you don't need to worry about the coming days. They go very fast and it becomes rather easy to sit. This is a natural process and, especially for people who are sitting this sesshin for the first time, I'd like to encourage you not to quit.

I always feel this kind of sitting practice is like the root of a tree, or foundation of a building, very invisible. It's supposed to be invisible. Nothing very splendid happens, even if I begin with, "Something has to happen because I have to change my messy life situation. This is the last chance!" But against my expectation, what it is, is tremendous pain. If we concentrate on smoothing our breathing, it becomes very hard to breathe, and gets stuck somewhere in the chest or throat. If we push it hard many times, the head begins to feel dizzy. If you are taught to count your breaths, it doesn't succeed. You always come to five, to seven, and you are wandering off the track, and, very ashamed, you come back to one. Finally you get to ten and feel you made it. Then the next one doesn't come. To do such a simple thing is very hard.

This living human being, human body, contains burning energy. This must be the reason we experience pain. When you touch a hot thing, you say, "Ouch!" When a burning flame comes close, you say, "Oh, it hurts!" When your life is facing the same kind of intensity, that must be what causes pain. Buddha's first sermon was "All beings are nothing but pain." He is saying life, itself, is in pain. He is not looking down from a high, peaceful place at the suffering people below. Many of his fellow practicers were old friends, whom he encouraged to look into the reasons for each painful experience.

Personal Problems

Beyond the physical pain of sitting, there is always more pain, which we don't need to call pain, but a sort of fog or cloud of a question. It is something which you know about, but don't know quite how it arose. We call these "problems," or unresolved matters, which get our attention. They are very attractive and impossible to let go. You think if you solve them, something important will arise within you. First, you are puzzled, "I don't understand that," or, "I cannot see through it." Teaching appears like that. Lots of koans are like that. There are hundreds of questions in the Old Testament and New Testament of the Bible. There are lots of koans in the Koran. Such questions let you pay attention to expanding your mind. Your religious spirit, no matter what tradition you have come from, will carry you through this time.

Basically, we have no problem, but having the right attitude to carry on our life is very important. "Right attitude" may be symbolized in your mind in language, or some other symbol. But if I ask, "What's the most important thing for you?" each person will answer, "I think, I feel, (whatever it is) is most important." That is what attitude is. It's the purpose of your present life. It's not something that somebody, or your teacher, said, so you go with it. It's not like that. Often your own basic compass may be expressed in the same language as others, but, for you, it really exists somewhere in your body/mind.

All of us have some knowledge of the reasons for our problems. Even though we may be used to knowing what to do, what to choose, if we get stuck and can't decide what to do or which way to turn, the pain comes. One kind of painful situation occurs when you cannot say "yes" or "no" when someone asks you for help. If you answer, "Yes, I can help you" or "No, I can't help you," then you have no problem, no pain, because you've already decided on one way among many choices.

In the case of relationships, we have been conditioned to want a long relationship with another being, instead of a temporary one. Instead of a transient life, we want eternal life; instead of continuous pain, we want a joyful, pleasant life; instead of nothing, we want to have something. Those are the impossible things we want while what is possible is all the things we don't want. So Buddha was a "twisting" teacher. Instead of promising eternal life, he pointed out how fragile, how transient and how impossible is the life we have got. We see that instead of eternal, joyful, unchanging conditions in life, we have continuous change. Even if our highest, deepest intellect reaches to the essence of our life, alas, we feel we cannot reach life, itself. This kind of pain is like a person who has no money and wants to be a millionaire. But if you have millions and billions in reserve, the fear of losing it, even one penny of it, or the fear of a shadow coming through the darkness to take it away from you, creates tremendous pain. If you are medium rich it is the same. You want more. And yet, here we are, feeling pretty good, actually. Having nothing, you feel pretty good. Having a lot, more than you need, you feel pretty good. That's pretty good!

Dualism

A human being is a very complicated existence. From ancient times we have been struggling with dualism, which can be described as the recognition of our reality at the same time as we long for perfection. Dualism is the split between reality and our ideals. We always face both. There are always two paths in front of you, and when you take one the other disappears. Then again two paths appear. In Indian Buddhist thinking the samsaric duality, the mundane world and the ideal world, always appears, and no path is seen between the two. In a book where you see heroes in the samsaric world, and darkness and brightness fighting each other, finally brightness wins. In Nietsche's Zarathustra, "Superperson," a similar idea of bodhisattvahood is seen. Instead, often in our own experience, we may feel that sitting only brings us questions instead of answers. But if you settle on an answer, and feel that is the end of your questioning, that is not so good. You find you have to let go of your vigorous effort to maintain purity, because with purity, dry simplicity comes, where there is almost no life. You become a closed system, all blocked off. In that closed system, when noise or a chaotic situation comes, you try to block it off. In other words, a cushion can be very soft at first, but it gets harder and harder and harder. Maybe you need a better cushion! Instead, you remember your bodhisattva nature, and over and over again you plunge into the suffering world without hesitation.

When you look into the dialectic, "yes or no" and go beyond it, "right or wrong" and go beyond them, that is how to solve the dilemma of two truths. Buddha's sitting is beyond pure and impure, holy and unholy. It is not something you understand. It's indescribable. If you explain it, it becomes something which you don't know yet, and yet when you are experiencing sitting with all of us, that understanding is here with you.

The Armies of Mara

When Buddha was recovering from the hard tapas practice, he found some munja grasses, tied them together and knit them, making something like a zabuton and zafu. At midnight of the first night, armies of Mara came to destroy him. There are nine different kinds of Mara: Desire, all kinds of desire, and also fear, as well as the endless thirst of love, and doubt. Illusion is another kind of Mara, when you get a little vain and begin to think you are different from other people. Mara is not something frightening, a fierce warrior who comes to cut your neck and split you in half. Rather, Mara dwells in the unknowing being which is you, and in the end you are completely lost. Nowadays we can say those are internal realizations. But when you read Buddha's biography, you believe it could be true, that some people came to him from "out there." The story is that Mara later confessed that Buddha was unable to be tricked. He followed him as soon as he left home, for seven years, but ended by saying, "I'm like a useless crow who picks at the rock. My beak is all bloody. Buddha is like a rock. Arrows cannot penetrate him."

Mara's temptation is something very familiar in our experience. The more we try hard, striving toward perfection, or toward a goal, the more the opposite force occurs. When you climb a mountain, toward the peak, the hardest climb occurs. When you dive in the ocean, you go to your limit and you feel like dying before you start to come up again. Desire to succeed, we experience naturally. We get hungry when we don't eat for some time. Hunger tells of the desire for food. This life has many needs without which it cannot be sustained. Without sleep an army of exhaustion, dullness, denseness, sleepiness, comes. That is Mara. Without sleep, we can hardly recover life. Without food we can hardly sustain this life. Without sexual desire, we are unable to continue generations. Without being known by others, we cannot sustain this life. Nothing is wrong with these needs, so we have a great army within us. What shall we do?

We are always in this dilemma: If we don't take the flesh of another existence, another life, into this body, there is no opportunity of living long. What do you give in return? What goes out? What takes you, so to speak? Fasting feels like the experience of not taking life into you, meaning you are eating yourself. The end of taking life is obvious, it is the end of this body. One month, forty days, must be the maximum length of fasting.

Chapter 4

Finding Yourself

"Most of you experienced the feeling of passing by the ridge of the high mountain by this time, the fourth day of sesshin. At the same time, you feel kind of lost, and sort of too much loosened up. You gave up thinking about yourself so much junk. Many of you dropped off those things, I think. A few of you are still working on them, because they seem not to go away."

Discover Your-Own-Self

Somewhere Dogen Zenji mentioned that to study the whole way of Buddha is nothing but to discover your true self––your own, not some other. This your-own-self, each of your-own-selves, is the key to the Buddha's way. Furthermore, Dogen says, to study and get to know yourself, or to truly become yourself, is to forget yourself. This process of religious dynamics almost reverses the search for Buddha, to come back to your daily self. Your daily self is the only existence. I mean, as experiential truth, nobody can thoroughly take over your life.

Some people devote their life to a teacher, and find that, without any struggle, when they do so, the teaching reveals their own truth. Devotion, an expression of utter trust, with no doubt, is very hard, and yet, I can say to you that whenever you learn earnestly, you always take this trusting attitude. All learning from a teacher points to one reliable teaching which the historical Shakyamuni Buddha left to his people, to each of us. It is, "Take absolute refuge in your own self. Depend on your own self." That is the only reliable island in the stormy ocean. Existence is like a little island in the stormy ocean. You, yourself, are an island.

Dualism as Skillful Means

There have been many centuries of discourse about whether human nature is essentially good or essentially hopelessly bad. You could argue either way. Someone said that to appreciate a good thing, you show an example of a bad thing. Is that right? The human condition is very much arranged to reveal constant dualism, and the continuous struggle of living is an example. This is a dilemma unless we realize that this dualism is prepared for the sake of skillful means. On one hand, we want to become all-sided, all-knowing existences. And on the other, we eternally want to keep the secret of our self. You don't want to be known by anybody, not because of sinfulness, or your many errors, but to remain in a pure, unknown state. Yet you want to know everything about everything and everybody. We go back and forth, knowing that in the end we have to give up everything. We know that it's best to keep light-bodied, light-minded, very close to zero, but before that we want to have everything. Before you lose everything, you want to have everything. Isn't that strange? The more you strive for purity, the more the realization of yourself is hopeless, helpless, an unreachable, stained realization. The countless contradictions within us are examples of dualism. What shall we do?

Everybody knows that seeking your own peaceful spirit is up to your own practice, and it's a way to learn how to live, which means you accept yourself totally as you are. Everybody wishes to be a truly satisfactory person, satisfactory to yourself, but this doesn't happen by hearing somebody say how well you do things or how wonderful you are. You will never be satisfied until you say, "yes" to yourself. Way-mind comes from that area. Each individual has spent many lifetimes' effort just to reach this life. You are continuing this effort, as the last chance to see how far you can go toward your own self. That kind of self we have got, each of us.

Sitting Still

Sitting is a sort of forgotten ability of humankind. You know what I'm talking about. When our survival was in danger, in ancient times, this was our main activity. Among all kinds of dangerous animals or poison foods, we had to keep our sense organs still, in order to find our position in the danger. We had internal awareness of what kind of food was good and what kind of food wasn't good. Now, after eating, we have to contemplate where those foods came from and where they went. We had many, many centuries of training, natural training. But nowadays we don't know who we are, in a very essential sense. We have become very sophisticated, very elaborated, in a cultural sense. And at our stage of blood mixture, we are also very different from ancient people. We have many life-traditions in our blood, in each individual existence, so the ancestral lineage is sort of hard to retrace. We have many roots to recall, to know where we are now, and where we will be in the future, as well as where our mind impulses will reach on this earth.

Even remembering these roots, we have a wonderful opportunity to make time to sit in zazen, without trying too much to know who we are or what we are doing, what we are supposed to be achieving. We don't pay much attention. A judgment of oneself upon each sitting is absolutely not necessary. Yet enormous effort goes into the sitting, which shows you are giving up self-centered choice of your activities. In doing so, you find you are accepting yourself as you truly are. You are giving room for "evil," so to speak, to exist around you. It's not always there, but you are giving some room for a chance that you might be evil. You can even question, "Maybe my whole entire life is just a little waste, or something." Now you have room to observe your short life, your short life-dynamic, among so many living existences. And you can also observe what good you can do for yourself and all existences around you. This is a very important time.

Sitting still is like a person who just shot an arrow and senses the arrow is moving alright. It's left from your realm, but you sense it's running well. Stillness is like that. In the stillness you see that the intuitions you are sensing are going alright. You are facing yourself. Sitting does nothing to you, but it reflects everything you have, not just a shadow of you but what you are. So when you fall into anxiety or self hatred, you become extremely clear about it. For a long time I thought that sitting still for many, many years of practice causes compassion or wisdom to be created. But it isn't so. Compassion and wisdom is what we are originally, and specks of misunderstanding, illusory knowledge about yourself, cause you to forget. Sitting is returning to what you are, actually, and what you are is discovered in sitting, by you, nobody else. Some people might say, "What is causing that person to become so strange?" But you are becoming your good, your closest friend who you wanted to meet.

This sesshin is giving you time to open up yourself, to include ancient times and the contents of all times, until today. The previous lives of our ancestors are coming through in our studies, helping us to know who we actually are. But we cannot stay there. We have to go one step ahead, because we are always one step ahead of those findings. We are tremendous manifestations, in this space, of many lives, constantly changing, no matter whether we know it or not. These lives are part of your urge to live, why you want to continue living. So, instead of going to the movies or traveling, you chose to sit. I don't know if it's good or bad, but it's a rare choice you made.

Chapter 5

Limitless Trust

"...asking why we have come to this world, and for what purpose our existence is shaped as a human body and mind. Trusting your own self, as well as giving full trust to others, is really, really hard."

Trust

During the last few nights we discussed a very core issue of our practice, facing our own self, asking why we have come to this world, and for what purpose our existence is shaped as a human body and mind. Trusting your own self, as well as giving full trust to others, is really, really hard. In your attempt to sit in one spot for hours and hours, day after day, there must be something you are working on. It is not a trifling matter. You are not a resting bird on a tree branch. You are not simply resting for a while on the cushion.

Trust is contained in sitting. Stillness is another way to express what trust is. For example, if you are lying down in bed, imagining that you are on a mountain waiting to be hit by lightening, but you Trust is contained in sitting. Stillness is another way to express what trust is. For example, if you are lying down in bed, imagining that you are on a mountain waiting to be hit by lightening, but you do not trust that you can face death that way, you will immediately jump up from the bed and run away from the lightening. But this lightening was in your imagination. Actually, this life we are experiencing day by day is not something in your imagination, nor does it turn out just as you have imagined it would. In stillness, day after day, you have a new opportunity to see yourself. Many, many new things happen, new people and things come into your life. They make an impression on you, and thus you are carried on, to the next day and the next.

Without giving your loving mind, your trusting mind, it seems no life remains. Living in this universe all alone, even in perfect knowledge, still doesn't satisfy you. The last word Dogen Zenji spoke on this was, "...forget yourself." This was not just a denial of yourself, as in, "I'm no good. I'll just forget myself." It's not like that. As I have said, you go into a different perspective of yourself, maybe you give yourself a broader room. Forgetting yourself, and trusting, at this point, feels the same to me. To forget oneself is, with knowledge, to give up your human way of perceiving things, and give more room to see what is actually happening to your own self and to all other existences. When you forget your small self the whole universe appears.

When we talk about trusting, about believing in something, or faith in something, we tend to think about this with a flavor of religion or a spiritual way. And yet, when you look into your daily activity, helping others, taking care of children or sick people, or working on making something for many, many days, you begin to understand what it means to have faith, or trust. There is great power in it. The word, "power," is probably not suitable, but the capacity to merge one's life force around or within others, is what I am talking about. An example would be if a person were to accidentally fall into a fast-flowing river, and everyone panicked, wanting to go in, but looking at the tide of dark water, they immediately identified themselves with the person who is floating away. "That's me! If I go in, I would be just like that!" The power, or belief, is when one who knows how to swim such a current, without hesitation, without fear, just jumps in and tries to add their force to this sinking force. Deep knowledge about things, and skills trained into your system, are the contents of your belief, or confidence.

I am talking about limitless, ceaseless trust. Otherwise, nothing happens. You are just sitting on a merry-go-round, eternally waiting for something to happen. Let's go back to Dogen Zenji saying, "To meet with your true self is to forget yourself." As long as your brain is entangled, your knowledge is entangled with your own self-dynamic, inside of your skin, you are still a blind man. I mean that your state is still in utter darkness, so that there is no way to identify yourself to anything or anyone. Other people are utter strangers. Animals are kind of ghost-like, wind-like creatures to you. You have no feeling about them. In such a state, even if you feel you are a very fine human being, a pretty good shape of a human being, still you are alone in this universe. It is like the state of Dr. Faust in Goethe's Faust.

Where does trust begin? Trust is certain knowledge, without listening to others, an intuitive field. Without speech you understand others, empathize with others. Even if you cannot take the place of another, you are able to reflect others' experience within yourself. In other words, this is identification of yourself and others, and the differences between you. It is not a state of guessing, or an analytical conclusion by which you understand others. It is immediate understanding of others.

In this busy, heated, fast society we often feel helpless in our effort to trust people and situations. We need to remember our trust doesn't depend on outside circumstances. Over and over again we encourage ourselves to fully trust others and feel satisfied instead of worrying about some kind of return from the other end. This has something to do with determination that no matter what the others' condition is, you decide to continue to trust. Looking closely, we understand that there is a deep satisfaction in trusting others. Perhaps this involves ignorance, so-called "blind trust" given toward others. It goes only one way.

Faith and Confidence

Faith, in the Judeo-Christian tradition, doesn't belong to a human being. It comes from God. It is a kind of setup of an incomplete one approaching the complete one, a very heavily stained one approaches the purest one. There is a deep feeling of wrongness, guilt. Everybody has had this feeling when we did something we shouldn't have done. Before doing it you felt, "I'm doing something wrong, and yet I have to do it." And then, later, "See, it was wrong!" And guilt pokes your heart. In Buddhism, the first way you identify yourself as a Buddhist is to believe in yourself, utterly. That is the first step. If that doesn't exist, nothing can work out. Enlightenment is not the issue here. Enlightenment is just a shadow. It's just an occasion. It appears and it goes away. You cannot have it. Faith is a dynamic manifestation of your own life, moment after moment. To have doubt about it is the most sinful thing, so to speak. Not knowing everything about your life is fine, but to doubt about it is the first mistake. Faith in oneself occurs even in total confusion.

It has been said that the great ocean of Buddhadharma, the truth in awakening, is entered by faith. "Shin" is the word in Japanese. The Chinese character shows "person" on one side and on the other side is the word "logos." "Person's logos." Usually we don't even question what "shin" is, what belief is, what trust is. Unknowing, we all admit that each of us exists. Don't you? That's what the feeling of "shin" is. You trust you are present here, and other people are present there. When children start to walk toward some high bars to play on, mother and father cannot bear to watch. And yet, parents really have to trust that nothing wrong will happen. What do you call that kind of mind which you give to others? Is that belief? What do you say? "I have faith in you, confidence, trust." So Buddhadharma is understood on this level. There is some kind of very powerful entity there with which you and others can meet.

Buddha's Final Advice

After his enlightenment experience, and his decision to live among people, Buddha lived another thirty-five years. He taught that he was just walking the path of he ancient Brahman's way, as taught in the Aryan tradition, the path of unity of Brahman and Atman. In the Vedic teachings, Atman is relative, Brahman is absolute, and the experience of their unity is a mystic experience. Buddha said, "I am not the first person. There were many Buddhas, Tathagatas before me. There will be many after me." At the age of eighty he passed on. The last journey he took was to go to an area where he used to visit, through many, many villages toward the north, and he would say, "What a wonderful time I had in this village!" At Kusinagara, he received his last meal from a disciple. The last thing he taught was that this body deteriorates into elements, so without being lazy or waiting for tomorrow, he asked his followers to do their best every moment. Speaking to those gathered around his death bed, he said, "Practice earnestly to realize that which is happening to everybody. It is occurring every second, to everybody, every being, as long as they exist. It is occurring every place, everywhere."

Even now, the Buddha's image is not clear. I cannot hear his voice so clear. But today we are very fortunate to have rather complete translations of Buddha's words, like Sutta Nipatta, and Dhammapada. About one hundred years after Buddha passed away, people started to put these materials together. When I read the last words of Buddha Shakyamuni to his disciples, telling them to trust themselves, telling each to depend on his own self as the original Buddhadharma, and to trust the Sangha, the fellow practicers, these words struck me so much. He is saying that unless you put them into practice and find truth in them, you don't need to trust even a well-known, famous teacher's words. Then he said, "I am passing away, and it is time to ask your last question. Do not hesitate, even if you are a newcomer. Time is swift." He talked to even a brand new person like that. "If you are too shy to ask, ask your elder to present your words." He encouraged people like that. So now we come here to sit because we are sure there is something in this very interesting, mysterious existence, a strange miracle.

Chapter 6

Buddha Tathagata

"So, Tathagata means 'thus come and thus gone,' at the same time. Again, it's very hard to capture. You are listening to continuous sound, but each sound you are capturing is what truth is. It is like the rhythm of continually running water."

Tathagata

After he started to recover, Buddha had a psychic experience in which Brahman appeared in his sight and requested that he must live long and relate with people. When he came back to those old tapas friends, every one of them gradually started to welcome him. One by one they accepted him in the circle. At that time Buddha said, "Do not call me 'you'." I ask myself what kind of mind gives that response that Buddha gave? It's natural to say, "How are you? How do you do?" But when he reappeared among people he never again said, "I believe," or "I think." Always he said, "Tathagata speaks." "Tathagata" refers to the one who accomplished the purpose, the one who has come:

"An unsurpassed, penetrating and perfect Dharma is rarely met with even in a hundred thousand million kalpas. Having it to see and listen to, to remember and accept, I vow to taste the truth of the Tathagata's words." (from a San Francisco Zen Center handout)

We struggled to translate this stanza into English around twenty years ago, and we ended up with a strange English stanza. It is hard to understand "Tathagata." The Buddha spoke of the "Tathagata" as his synonym, and when he referred to former Buddhas he would say, "So and so Tathagata." "Yaweh" is the closest word to this "Tathagata." It means it is complete in itself, and no words are able to describe what it is. Tatha means "thus," "as," "it," "as a thing is," "as things are." Gata is "has come," so you are experiencing "it." At the same time this same word, agata, means "gone." Thus you are able to see the other side of "it." So, Tathagata means "thus come and thus gone," at the same time. Again, it's very hard to capture. You are listening to continuous sound, but each sound you are capturing is what truth is. It is like the rhythm of continually running water.

Shakyamuni Buddha, himself, said, "Myself and great earth... sentient beings... same time accomplished the way." It's not that Buddha became a conqueror, and the rest of us are all still straying somewhere. Everything became "accomplished."

So one view of it is that each one of you is a jewel in Indra's net, and the next person is a jewel, and all beings are placing themselves in Indra's net. No two are the same. It must certainly be so, otherwise I could not understand who each of you are, or why you are here. Once, twice, we meet, maybe five or ten years between. And still we remember, "Oh, yes, we met a long time ago," and you recover your precise memory of what happened.

The contents of the enlightenment experience are the same as this "Tathagata." It rejects your knowing, because it exists in the root of the action of knowing. The one who knows is what it is. The one which is known by it is not necessarily what it is. This "Tathagata" is what your real essence of life is, what truth, itself, is, so that we become very helpless when we try to know it. The knowledge of our existence, what we are, what things are, is a kind of ancient memory of what it is. We wish to experience the past as the present, and as we experience the past, nothing is known about the future. In terms of knowing about the future we are in helpless darkness.

Buddha is nobody else but each of us.

This week to enjoy sesshin is about to come to an end. As I told you, it is not so difficult, is it? But a lot of things happened. They are invisible. Something sat with you. You have seen about one hundred movies, maybe. You have seen so many things. I don't want to say you should just forget those movies. The one who watches and keeps letting the whole thing happen is a very important part of yourself. It is not necessarily a judging function, just an observing one. You already know that to study Buddha's way is to study yourself. This is not something unfamiliar to you. It is the sole concern you have carried and are still working on all the time. Buddha is nobody else but each of us.

There are many ways to understand Buddha's presence in our lives. When you experience your own child's birth it becomes clear that mother, father and immediate relatives have totally awakened this little new life which has just arrived. If you are the mother, you cannot tell what it is, but certainly it is a definite, brand new life which came through you, as if destroying your being. Life is like that. It's up to you to define it, but when you look into your own life from birth until today, something has been continuing to survive, continuing to manifest. You may say it's just a wind-like life force, yet you keep your identity from birth until your death day. Gathering all elements, body and mind function somewhat together. We all know this life phenomenon of us is short, and when the time comes, all elements scatter again.

Life Force

Day and night, day and night, the heart beats regularly, whether or not you are aware of it. The breathing continues with a certain rhythm. Your sense organs function amazingly, and brain, eyes, hands, which way you move every moment, are all spontaneous. These are taken care of in a split second. What kind of life is it? Do you call it a human being? In the Buddhist custom, we don't name it human. It is simply life, and with surprise and amazement we call it Buddha nature. This is the total dynamic of awakening nature. This life force is seeking an object to love. "Love," in this case, means "give something of yourself." Legs move you, compassion drives you to move toward the object. When you see a knowledgeable, experienced person, naturally you feel deep admiration, causing a magnetic pull toward that person. When you start to observe such impulses, you finally find out what are the contents of this magnetic force. When you see somebody suffering in pain or illness, immediately you go closer to find out what you can do for this person. The same life force makes you want to share your knowledge and wisdom. All beings have inborn Buddha nature.

Chapter 7
Sesshin

"... My greatest, most exciting experience is to sense this practice here as something utterly new to me."

Coming Together

My greatest, most exciting experience is to sense this practice here as something utterly new to me. Each of you is certainly different from any Japanese or Indian or Tibetan. It is a great thing to see. And sometimes it makes me very scared, as if all of you are newly arrived aliens, hard to communicate with. Genetically, you originated on this earth, so I feel alright, but I cannot understand the mind tradition you have carried through in successive life continuations. I cannot understand what memories you contain in your body and mind. It is very strange to think about what caused you to sit here without question. I finally conclude that we are participating in religious anarchy. Everybody has their own unique belief, and I feel very good about it. But to communicate with each other is really hard. The wonderful thing is, when we sit and live together for a few days, without question we accept each other. Without asking others about what's in their mind, we can sense where people are. We have such a wonderful ability to observe.

Kensho

You have heard of "kensho." "Ken" means "perceive," "sho" is the nature of things. Kensho means that while you struggle between the ideal self, and this limited poor thing which is here, they are actually one. They are not uniting or becoming one. It was originally one, and it is always one. That realization is the usual experience of kensho. It does not happen just once. In one way or the other, every one of us has had such an outrageous experience. Otherwise, I don't think you would be here.

You don't go anywhere from kensho. Seeking to know yourself ends, and time starts. The future doesn't exist in the future, and the past hasn't gone yet. Your ordinary dualistic knowledge of everything ends. But you don't dwell in such a realization. After the second or third moment, you discover you are still a person, and you get up and prepare yourself for the day as usual. You live as if nothing has happened. You still get mad, and you get glad when something good happens. But each time, when you realize this original self within you, the battle within you somewhat ends. In a sense, the battle to actualize such oneness starts anew. It is a real battle. Other existences out there are not others any more, so that the problem is much more serious when you see suffering people. That becomes your own suffering, immediately. Or when someone is experiencing great joy, by looking at, hearing, that joy, you become so happy!

Now you know what trusting others is. By itself, this trust reunites the separate pieces of yourself, yourself and others. Dogen Zenji says, "Body and mind of one's own self, body and mind of others' own selves, drop off... to be conveyed by all myriad dharmas." So realization is not just your own realization about the identification of your own self and others' own selves. Unique differences between yourself and others are perceived, still. But along with that awareness, one's own self, body and mind, and others' own selves, bodies and minds, are cast off.

What kind of understanding is it? You experience this during and after trusting each other and then recovering independence. It goes like, "You are actually myself," you say to any single thing, or even any abstract existence. You say, "You are nothing but myself, but I am not you. I am not yourself." And the same words you hear from another person about yourself. The other person says, "Oh, you are myself, but you are not my self. Is that so?" "Yes, it is so." So complete identity, and what was your original self both drop off, no conversation necessary, and what remains is who you are. That person is who you are. Nobody has been like yourself.

Embracing Mind

What "sesshin" means is "embracing mind." Whoever is sitting, that person's mind embraces the whole situation, centered in that person. So you have full responsibility and full understanding, by yourself, of what sesshin means to you. The teaching is within you, which includes how you live, how you think, where you came from. Memories arise, memories of your experiences are always there, no matter whether you deny them or accept them. Nothing is missed, nothing is needed to be changed in you, as you are. You actually are living how it should be although there is no such "should." Even the effort to become Buddha, you set aside. In one sense this is a terrible state! It's the hardest kind of operation. You do it to reveal your own truth, no matter how fragile, how uncertain. You place your own life dynamic on the cushion.

"Embrace mind" means that the five skandhas, mind and physical quality, are fully functioning. As you notice, this physical existence is very dynamic, a living thing which you cannot stop because it goes by itself. Time passes, contents change. Maybe the contents are living things, who go by themselves, and you are that which is experiencing and feeling them. In everyday life we do not have this kind of fully stretched mind. You feel this if you meditate every day, and then go out to join people. You really notice it when one day you do not sit, but just go to work. You really notice something is different. When sesshin ends and you go to everyday life, you feel very strange. The speed of activities seems like a fast-forwarding movie, and yet you also notice it is some kind of trick of your mind. This kind of change appears right after the closing remarks of sesshin. Like a treasure box you open, and start to dump out the treasure. Endlessly you talk. You'll see this afternoon. But that is a small part of it. The effect of sesshin usually continues for about a month, and then you feel you are normal again. Then you start to hear, "Sesshin is coming again!" Some people refer to Zen people as "sesshin addicts."

Goodbye

When you go back where you came from and become invisible from my sight, I wish my mind could go with each one, to help you be strong and not get destroyed. The spirit can be destroyed by many, many difficulties and that's why I talk about faith in yourself, in your own life, which is pretty short. But if you become very proud of yourself without any reason, that's the biggest pit you can fall into, even if you feel great, because, phenomenally, you feel the teaching seems to be going very well. If practice doesn't touch the key point, the core, this can be an illusory enjoyment. Individuality, for which reason you were born, and also misunderstanding of individuality and independence, are very dangerous things. The key point is confidence within you about your true nature.

When the ferry boat arrives on the other shore, you say, "Goodbye," to the other passengers, and don't know when you are going to meet again. If this practice together is not touching the key point, it's all my fault! And it's all your foolishness, so it's very serious.

ROHATSU SESSHIN

SESSHIN

ASSEMBLY ON THE ENLIGHTENMENT OF BUDDHA

Chapter 8

Sitting Practice

"Sitting is the action of going into Buddha's World"

Sitting Practice

Buddhism grew out of the enlightenment experience of Shakyamuni. We don't know exactly what his experience was, but evidence of Buddha's experience comes from the basic teaching that our refuge is our own experience. So our teacher, Dogen Zenji, advised us that the way of the Buddha is discovering your own self.

Even though the desire to sit is a kind of imitation of the historical Buddha, many Buddhists do not do this practice. Actually most Buddhists don't sit in zazen. They think it is conceited, taking the attitude, "You think you can do the same thing as Buddha." But from my search for what kind of teaching Buddha gave, the teaching is, even today, that if you say you cannot sit, that's a conceit. Not to feel that the importance of your life is as important as the historical Buddha, that is a conceit. You don't condemn your life by merely observing the helpless state of your own self. Life is absolutely rare. We really miss out if we misunderstand what our life is. You misguide yourself and you cannot go to the destination you are supposed to walk to. It would be too bad to go to your destination in the coffin, or if somebody else carries you to your destination.

Remembering the advice of Dogen Zenji, it is said that in order to admit and observe exactly how you are, sitting in zazen is the best way. Nobody can tell you what you have been; you have to see it yourself, what you have gotten and how things are going. You naturally see. That is the beginning. But a lot of problems continue to go along with our life. It is truly strange to be born as a human being. Maybe to be something else, like a rock or dewdrop or something, would be a little easier. Every day somewhere hurts. There is something wrong every day. But the wonderful thing is, certainly something is new every day, although we cannot say quite what it is. But something is new. That new thing must be something we already knew but had always forgotten. It's essential characteristic is to allow us to live another day.

Once in a while we gather like this for longer and more intense sitting practice. Our reasons depend on each of us since every one of us manages daily life in a different way. People who sit every day do not find it so difficult to start to go deeper, but for people who do not or cannot sit every day, the beginning of sesshin is a sort of hard way. It takes some time to adjust your body and mind. Determination to spend a week or so pushes you to find your sitting place, but many pieces of your life are still out there, causing concern about how you put the whole thing together. I hope it's only me. I always leave lots of things unfinished. But since we came here and stopped running around, we can let all those things work together.

When I join with people in sitting, my intention is to open this sitting opportunity to everybody who is ready to do it, but it is important to avoid the problem of wrong sitting. If you spend a week sitting, in vain, it's my problem. I don't want you to waste your precious time. We spend one third of our life sleeping, literally sleeping. When you are awake, you eat and do other things you are not quite sure you want to do, for maybe another third. That leaves one third to do what you decide to do. For some indescribable reason you have an urge to meditate. You want to find out what it is. No one can solve this puzzle for you, so you need to make time to face it. The most important thing is not zazen, but the person doing it. If you always do it and don't know why you do it, that's a problem.

The technique of sitting meditation is very simple. The first thing is a will to sit. You think, " I'd like to sit. It is time to sit." Before the body gets into a sitting position, you are already feeling it. Walking toward the place where you are going to sit, or be, you are arranging the space. The physical arrangement, and also the spiritual and mental arrangement gradually come together, before the actual sitting. The techniques are to move quietly, sit still, and have calm breath. That's all. The problems are the various attachments and interests which take us away from meditation. We see many cases where people are afraid to meditate. For them, to go back to the very first exciting movement toward stillness is frightening, but you don't need to feel this fear.

If you feel good about your zazen, that's good, so continue. But if you don't feel good about your zazen you're doing something wrong. Maybe your posture is not good. Posture is very important and it's all of your zazen you have to show. So train your posture. You cannot see breath but it is a mark of invisible life, so find life under the breath. It's always there. Do not be caught up in what kind of breathing you are doing; just breathe naturally. Also, mind sits when life sits, so you observe it as it is. Do not be caught by valuing or evaluating.

Anybody can sit when they're ready to sit. The urge or interest in sitting can occur to anybody, anytime. My deep wish is that it can be adapted to any religion, so I hope this sitting does not have too much structure around it. But this formal sitting, as you sit, should be polished by each person. It can be very powerful and joyful action when you come to the point you physically trained for. It feels like your destination is reached, your search is ended. It doesn't end, but you feel that. At that point you don't look around for somebody else's opinion, you just feel very confident about what you are doing, and about yourself.

When Buddha sat on the seat of conquering evil, he was confronting the question of life or death, whether to continue to live, or end his life, his practice, his search. We call it an attack of Mara. It is not Mara attacking from somewhere else; it's within you, so that you need a very strong sense of determination. Like Buddha's vision, a vision comes to you, of arrows of hatred, poisoned arrows coming at you, but they stop in space and fall away. Or lightening comes in the sky and it explodes and turns to blossoms and they land on the ground. These images symbolize the change that can happen in this struggle to find your own way.

But instead of just talking about what kind of sitting we are doing, rather, I would like to sit with you, and you also sit, and discover your own understanding of what sitting is, by yourself. It's impossible to teach the meaning of sitting. You won't believe it. Not because I say something wrong, but until you experience it and confirm it by yourself, you cannot believe it. After thirty years, on and off, sitting experience, I really feel that Dogen's statement is truly right, that sitting is the action of going into Buddha's world. In other words, because you are Buddhas, you can sit. It is either you going into Buddha's world, or Buddha appearing in the human world in human form. Looked at this way, your sitting is always your sitting.

Silence

Especially on the first day, the everyday pattern of life takes over my sitting. My body resists, my mind can be pacified but my resistant body does not want to sit down. It's hard to observe the whole thing, what's important and what's not important. Last night Ino said we should make an effort not to disturb others' "inwardness." I was puzzled. What is that "inwardness"? Yet we can somewhat understand what he meant by that word. Persons are all carrying a concentrated, invisible force. When people gather, these different kinds of vibrations come close and merge. Naturally, we respond to these vibrations, so this keeping silence, not talking about unnecessary things, is the nature of sitting practice, not a rule. Especially if you pay attention to movement before and after sitting as an extension of sitting, then you understand.

Kinhin

Kinhin is a very important practice here. As mentioned by Dogen Zenji's teacher, Nyojo Zenji, the speed of kinhin can be described as when you see a person from a distance who is doing kinhin; you don't see movement, until one or two seconds later you see they changed position. Kinhin is that kind of slow and soft movement. When you do kinhin with a very aware mind, you begin to notice that in everyday life we are always skipping that kind of space by getting up and immediately running. Or even before you get up and stand straight, you pick up something, or do something, immediately.

I used to watch older people's kinhin. To young people, old people's walk is very uncertain, but when you get into their physical condition and mind state, their stiffness, the step of their walk, is very different from our unaware walking. Ours is a sort of spinning walk, with no direction, while they may shake or wobble. When you walk very slow, if you are really awake and together from head to toe, very contented, and know the energy and weight of your body, you do not wobble. You feel that not only you are walking, but the world is walking with you. Old people's walking is toward a certain object, which encourages them to trust that, even wobbling, they are moving toward the object. Our wobbling is just wobbling. Do you know which direction you are walking? Obviously, during sesshin we walk toward another sitting and maybe the last step will be toward where you sat, toward where you really can be.

Facing the Wall

At first I didn't understand why we face the wall. I was taught that we do it because Bodhidharma did it, and the best way was to do as we were taught. If you questioned the teacher there was trouble as he was a very stubborn guy. Why do we face toward the wall when we do zazen? Gazing at the wall actually means we sit behind the wall. Zazen is not a game, or a show, to be seen by others, nor is it turning away or separating from the world. We face the wall to forget this small self and forgetting the self the whole universe appears. So the plain wall works as empty space, like a plain sky. When something happens in your mind, the wall is a screen.

Bodhidharma sat in front of a cave wall, but we don't know what he saw. We are not in a movie theatre waiting for the movie projector to start. You are the projector! Whatever comes to you, about the future, about the forgotten past, important and unimportant things, you stay in the present moment. For one second, one split moment, the wall is not there. If you were practicing archery, you would set the target and find a safe spot from which to send the arrow, but what you would observe is your physical dynamics, your balance, not the target. So I would say that the wall you face is not quite a wall, rather, it is a meeting with you. It's easy to see nothing is there. Instead of having a constant image of a teacher or friend, it's blank, to save you, reflect you. Your backside is open to all enemies, troubles, and everything. In other words, you show your back to the whole world.

Posture

I would like to talk about posture. It may be right to say that there is "right posture" for sitting. Many times during sesshin you hit that right posture and swing away from it, then go back to it. You begin to understand what right posture is for you. You can perceive it. It relates with how your mind state is at that time. Right posture in sitting creates the content of sitting, based on what you have been experiencing up to now. This requires detachment from your desire to do it, letting it happen by itself. Right posture does not mean you are doing sitting. Right posture, itself, is sitting, and your whole body system is going into that posture.

The physical posture we take in sitting is just a part of the whole posture. Many things meditate in that space. Speaking relatively, the outside world is there, where many things and people are living and changing. So we may feel, "I am here, the world is there, and I will go back there sometime." But why do you think you have retreated in sesshin? Or, if sesshin sounds like a trip, why did you go on a trip? Someone said, "Sesshin is like catching the right horse on the merry-go-round." This suggests that if you get on the horse that is going up and down, then you can't get off. So you think about how you are going to get off and get out of the merry-go-round without falling down. In one sense, sesshin is like that. Although you discover that you cannot change, and don't need to change, an important thing to know is that through practice there is an invisible change, which you don't recognize.

Your physical posture, year after year, becomes polished, and with repeated sitting, muscles become very refined. You begin to learn not to pull one part because it pulls your whole body, stretching a muscle so it cannot contract. Your muscles become very balanced so you are able to feel that almost nothing is there. Muscles, intestines and bones are there but you don't feel they are there. The object is a stretched spine, with the neck in line with the spine. When you slightly lean right, left, backward, forward, you can find which point is your straight posture, related to the incredible pull of gravity. A thousand million lines of this gravity pull you down. You swing your body and finally come to one point. But it doesn't continue that way. You again crumble down, so you have to again build it up. Maybe every twenty minutes or so you have to redo it.

The way to find your right posture is to focus your attention on your inner feeling. It's hard to say what this feeling is: Inner eye, inner ear, or inner sensation, which is able to observe every part of your body. If you are sitting cross-legged, if you can have the soles of your feet facing upward, pressing down on your thighs, it gives a deeply grounded sensation, on the earth, not flying purposelessly in the air. This is not an accidental discovery, rather it is a polished discovery. Whether you are sitting in lotus, half lotus, seiza, or in a chair, the spine, which is a pillar for your heavy head to sit on, and the upper body, have to be quite solid on your cushion. The waist bone, meaning the back bone behind your belt, maybe an inch lower, behind your center of hara, goes in, instead of out. When you do that, naturally the chest opens too much, so you let the chest go in, so air goes smoothly, instead of being pressured. Don't pull the chest in too much, but just to correct too much openness of the chest.

Begin to notice if your body is crooked when you are sitting. If you keep a crooked posture maybe in five years you will be a curved figure. You will begin to feel the tilted posture is the right posture, and when somebody comes to try to pull you back, you will feel, "I am falling down!" It is quite difficult to feel the right position of sitting. It's always crumbling down. The living body doesn't allow you to feel the position is perfect, and then criticism comes to you, "Zen sitting is too rigid." It takes strenuous effort to attain the right position and sustain the right form for yourself, like a ballerina standing on a toe for ten minutes. It might feel too rigid because it is a rare form for you. As an experiment, try to destroy your sitting. It's very easy to mess up your posture in this meditation by just rolling your eyeballs around, looking busily from here to there. Then go the other way around and come back to the still position of your eyes. Something opens up. This is what is meant by sitting still.

Keeping the mudra together is another effort. The mudra of *dharmadhatu* is giving up the state of discrimination and giving total trust to everything. That's what this mudra is. All fingers come together and become one thing. The mudra is the shape of a stupa, a limitless temple where all truth can dwell. You give up your own self-made dwelling. That's what a stupa is. You express your trust in this point of existence by not moving away for a while. The center of stillness is where you are. It is symmetrical. Head, shoulders, and legs do not tilt. When your head tilts, straighten it. Don't let your view tilt. Inside of your mouth, no air remains. Of course, you don't chew candy in it! You don't put anything in it. It is firmly closed, so air goes in and out through the nose.

From time to time, in your daily life, really make an effort to straighten your posture. Information is coming to your central inner sensations which is telling you whether or not you are well balanced. You may react to this information, saying, "I cannot stand this! I have to go somewhere and sit." Or you could have a sensation of agreement or disagreement with all your sense organs about where you are or how you are. So you find the right position, and then you have nothing to think about any more, nothing to bring up from any past or future. This is the present moment. Where you are, what you are, is there.

I speak of this zazen practice, not as a result of my intellectual analysis, but out of my deep respect and belief. I appeal to your intuition in picking up this practice in your life, which sometimes, especially for new people or older people, who have a problem sitting intensely, it appears very harsh. It is a hard practice to encourage, I know. But when the body finally is able to take the right posture, you sit as if no one is sitting there. At that time you feel yourself.

But we also know that our body is like a sand castle by the beach. We have to build it up, maybe every two or three minutes, checking every part of our body. Obviously, perfect posture is not the aim. More important is continuous effort and alertness.

Chapter 9

Problems, Pain

"...make room to feel what is called
"empathetic" understanding of how
others are feeling about themselves."

Problems

This is the second night. I understand all of us went through a very hard time today. With each sitting, whatever came into your mind turned to big problems. Maybe it is your own problem, a personal one, or beyond personal, yet still your own problem.

When you have been practicing for many years, quite seriously and earnestly, it looks like you have teachers and fellow practicers around, but you are basically still led by your own intuition. It has been the only way for you, I think. When I ask, "Any questions?" you keep silent, maybe because you realize you don't know what you are doing, where you are at, why you are doing it. On the second day of sesshin, you absurdly become a beginner again. Achievement, understanding, memories of your practice, have to be set aside in order to look at your life. You have to drop all conceptions about yourself. It's kind of hard to let go of them, especially when you feel you had understood something about this practice and what it does for your life.

As you know, real study cannot be like listening to a lecture. That's just a small part of study. Real study has to be like pounding, during time by yourself. It's like squeezing drops of juice, when a little bit comes out each time. This is your rare opportunity to confirm that your intuition is really true. There is much information available on TV, magazines, copied information, second hand, third hand, but it just makes your mind busy.

During sitting, you have memories of occasions, re-experiencing your past instants. You are able to become the audience, reexamining what they were, what was actually going on, until you are ready to observe one occasion correctly. Then the emotions start to unfold again. This kind of pain, or joy, is real, but actually it is not quite real. Conscious memories of your deeds, which are karma consciousness, and emotional reactions to them, are finished every moment. You observe them and accept them, letting them go. If you continue to stick onto some part of those experiences, you continue charging up your emotion every moment. This doesn't do any good. When we ask what it is which senses this suffering, we have to understand that the one who is breathing in and out, in and out, doesn't suffer. But it does sense suffering.

In daily activities we have almost no time to be really alone. We are continuously manifesting in relationships, in which things don't work as we planned or imagined. Day after day we are surprised that our activity has created so many fantastic things which we cannot afford to take care of. Maybe once in a while we sit for a short time, irregularly, and rarely really look at ourselves. We wish to be very wise, living this life in a very meaningful and useful way, but, alas, we know it is so difficult to be wise. We wind up in such situations, where it is hard to see what's going on. We don't know what's wrong with us. Although what's wrong with others, sometimes we can see!

Always in the second and third days of sesshin my cheeks become very hot because of so many embarrassing things I have done. I want to write or call to apologize to those for whom a difficult time was made. I feel I am so bad. Maybe it's my personal problem, but I'd like to talk about it a little bit. It is ceaseless self-clinging. "Gasshu" is the word, in Japanese Buddhist terminology. "Shu" is "cling." You stick on it, hang on it. "Ga" is "self." When we get into an uncomfortable situation, we like to go around it, not through it. We want to be safe and not be involved in the next messy situation which is obviously coming. When something nice happens I don't want to lose it, so I make every effort to keep it, make it last. When somebody else gets in trouble, feelings appear in me: "See, I knew that would happen," and, "It is nice it wasn't me," or something like that. These are unspeakable unconscious situations, which become very embarrassing when I see the whole situation and what I am doing. But if I don't take care of this, it will keep coming back on a larger scale, so in a corner of my mind

I always make room to feel what is called "empathetic" understanding of how others are feeling about themselves.

I really wish each sitting would broaden our perspective and let our mind and body be able to move, in any direction, with what is happening. I think this is what is meant by mind transcending and being able to embrace reality, finding out what is the best way to let a blocked situation unfold, finding the direction to move on, dissolving a situation or allowing it to flourish. I recognize that when I'm very busy every day, being concerned with so many things, one after another, my effort gets very shallow. My work is not effective in each situation, and day after day my concerns increase, so finally I come to realize I'm getting into a place in which I have no time to concentrate on what's most important for me, and what's the most important thing to do. Coming here, sitting with you, is very intense and pleasant, of course, and I am very glad that you have a chance to sit this amount of time, but in the corner of my mind there is a voice, "Is it alright?" These are my questions which I'm asking myself, and you, "How is your house? Who is taking care of your house? Is the house very messy? Isn't my wife hysterical about my absence, having to answer constant phone calls?" And there is also some feeling that it's alright. Whatever happens at home, it will go alright. It's not a wish, but a feeling that whatever happens, it will go alright.

Pain

We sometimes complain of pain in the legs, neck, or back. But know that pain is always there. You have just noticed it. It's not something you newly produced. Sometimes it shows up in other activities, such as when you walk on steep hills. When you stop climbing a mountain, the pain goes away, but you know it is still there. Although we call it pain, it is simply a force which came along with our existence. Maybe in this force there is always pain, if there is sense to feel it. When I touch my "nyoi" (stick) to the floor, both, my stick and the floor, feel pain, but they don't say so. When a new life is born, the intensity of that force lets the mother feel pain, along with incredible joy, which is another part of the pain. If you just see the good or pleasant part of an activity and avoid the pain, or avoid piercing cold or suffocating heat, then you are limiting yourself, not letting the force go from one end to the other. Even with pain, what happens in sitting is that the scale of your sensations gets smaller and smaller until finally you feel that you came to a painless place, a very comfortable place, not hot, not cold, not high, not deep, about a middle place. Then you discover there is incredible pain in there. Not being able to get out of it causes lots of pain again.

How is your sitting? I am feeling that you are starting to see the confused state of yourself, a clear figure of confusion. It's hard to know what to say about it. Sitting the whole day is a very difficult thing to do. As soon as you sit, your body begins to feel pain coming up from the bottom and toward the end of one sitting the whole body is in pain. What are we doing this for? Getting up is somewhat of a relief from pain, numbness and sleep, and about the time you get bored walking, again you have to sit and repeat the same thing again, and again, and again. It seems that zazen, sitting in a cross-legged position, unmovable, is prepared for us to feel pain. It is a different kind of pain from a sting or needle prick. You know it is going to happen and it surely happens, in hips and legs. I cannot pretend it doesn't happen. It happens. Standing up, bending, doing something in the same form for a long time, naturally gives us the same kind of painful situation. There is another feeling, a feeling that some kind of policeman is inside of you, judging your zazen. It is called "shinno shinjo." "Shinno" is "mind king." "Shinjo" is the realm of the king. The important thing is not to judge your poor effort in sitting, but simply encourage yourself to reach to the present, instead of directing yourself away. It's like a sailor sailing a boat in the storm. You have to be aware. But you also have to be aware that the storm is also yourself. You have to know why the storm is there, and how the boat stays on the surface of the waves. If you resist the storm, it's impossible to sail, I think. What I am saying is that your sitting, your body posture, is like a little ship. The storm is where we live, in this big world.

I wonder whether Dogen's words are true that zazen is the great "Dharma gate of peace and joy." Is that true? For a few minutes, in the beginning, we can agree. Sometimes you feel easy and peaceful in your sitting because there are no urgent impulses in your body. But it is often very painful to sit, worrying that you are not doing the things you are required to do in your daily life. These may feel like emergencies, but you have to really look at why you aren't doing all of them at once. Looking at these "emergencies" is the dynamic of sitting in this world. Even in one short sitting, a little "policeman" can also be a big helper for your sitting. In the past, some people prepared a sharp nail, put it in the cushion, and when unbearable drowsiness came to conquer them, pressed down to feel the pain, and woke up! Hakuin Zenji did that, as well as many others. And, in the monastery, the "kyosaku" is the "alert stick." It wakes you up. Sometimes it is used for punishment for small mistakes in the monastic life situation, but basically it is tapping on your body, saying, "You are drifting away. Come back."

I am afraid that everyone is experiencing tremendous pain. As soon as you sit on the cushion, about five or ten minutes, having a good time, here it comes. A lot of pain starts to be felt by your mind. Waiting for the kinhin bell, you have discovered what eternity means. It seems that being born as a human form of life has some very sacred meaning in not escaping, but digesting, our position in existence. Even if we sit like a rock, I am sure enormous pain is always there because of the rule of gravity. Having sensitivity embedded in our system is, in one sense, very wonderful, allowing us to know what's going on. In another sense, it is very inconvenient. You may begin to feel tremendous pain as some kind of signal not to push yourself too far, a signal which you are ignoring. In spite of all that I also know that many of you have already experienced sitting as not just a continuous fight with pain, because you have discovered that the other side of pain is the intensity of knowing where you exist. This realization gives you joy. If we didn't have this nerve system embedded in our body, we wouldn't know where we are, or what direction our body is facing.

We are in pain all the time. You can find it, endlessly, anywhere you look. But know that there is a way to find the right amount of it and have a good time. In sitting, even a slight move makes a very big change in your level of pain. When you contract your muscles, hold your body, tighten all your bones and then release them, you can adjust the amount of pain. It's not good to just sit still and look at that pain. Instead, you work with the muscles. When you lean back and sit on your butt only, the pain goes to the butt, so you ask your knees to help, letting the pain go into the ground. One important thing is to stretch your spine, not building it up from the tail bone, but you stretch by the muscle of your neck. At the same time your chest is opened up, not sunken. (On the other hand, if your chest is too opened, the air doesn't go through.) The spine is slanted, and you tilt the pelvis bone so your stomach comes out. The air should go straight down.

Pain is a big subject during sesshin and I feel sorry about it, but we have to look at it directly and work with it, work around it. Our mind, our being, always wants to achieve the supreme joy, and on the other hand, this dukkha, this suffering, follows with it. Because of pushing, the opposite force comes. By lifting, downward energy comes at the same time. When you want to practice intensely, many things appear as a hindrance to your practice. It's only when you want to practice that these hindrances start to come around and pull you down. We live in a world of strange rules, and we have to look at what's going on. Daily life is full of dilemmas, and in order to understand our human condition, we have to look at them. This is a very good subject to work on. When we begin to see which are necessary worries, unnecessary worries will disappear.

Psychological pain and physical pain happen not only in sitting, rather, intense involvement in something always causes a similar kind of pain. When mountain climbing gets very intense there is tremendous pain. You are exhausted and yet you cannot go back. The only way is up. The sensation you are feeling is gravity, and if it alone existed, you would not exist in that force of gravity, and there would be no problem. In this situation, to exist is to have pain. The mind in stillness also brings the problem of sensing pain as it is. To ignore it is not good. To avoid injury, observe what kind of pain it is. Some feel pain in kinhin. Even lying down for many days can be very painful. Sukha-dukha is Sanskrit for the opposite extremes of pain. Sukha is positive pain, which is joy. Dukha is negative pain, or negative joy, which becomes very intense when you do not want to have it. You swing between positive pressure and negative pressure.

The triangular sitting posture is very interesting. The shape of a pyramid is a very, very good form for containing force within it. A round shape is good, too, but unless some support exists, it rolls and you lose your stillness. If you lie down and begin to meditate, you finally go to sleep because your mind is able to melt down to the ground and nothing is left. This pyramid shape is the one which you take in sitting. A triangle is the form which pierces things. When it spins, you notice that it can be a drill, making a hole. We also know that this form, this human body, is a part of karmic force, meaning that without parents you wouldn't exist here, and without you, your children could not exist. In this sense, to have a body on this earth is a very karmic condition. Without this karmic condition you could not exist as the expression of "joriki," ultimate force.

But we have to discuss about unusual pain, beyond the normal pain in sitting. Leg pain shouldn't be pushed too much. For example, you might have torn the cartilage in your knee. Even so, the pain is not there, it's somewhere else, in your mind. The bigger problem is the big doubt in your mind as you are telling yourself, "If I continue five minutes more, maybe I won't be able to sit any more for a long time." That kind of worry is a bigger pain. You might need to have your knee x-rayed when the sesshin is over, to see what's in there. This is not a torturing room, so I encourage you not to push yourself, in spite of pain, toward a fine posture. Take the best posture you can, but you can sit any way, and you can also stretch your leg. Find some corner seat, and make room to stretch. The main point is to keep your upper body upright, from the end of your spine to the tip of your head, arranging your body in the force of gravity. You can fold your legs as you want. One recommendation for pain is to sit, not necessarily in full lotus, but in half lotus, seiza, or in a chair.

We are always in pain, in all parts, although when we are moving around we forget. If you keep your posture tilted for a long time, your pain is great. Try to stretch your arms out and hold them, unsupported, for five minutes; you will start to cry. It is not just pain, but a powerful grinding feeling, like screwing yourself into the ground. It's like a hot drill, boring in. A rocket burns when it goes very fast. Such a thing is happening to you, so keep good balance, as symmetrical as possible. For one or two sittings, you can take any kind of posture, but in long, intense sitting, the mind sits. That is a key point. After a while the mind becomes harder than ice, sometimes harder than a diamond, or the mind becomes hotter than boiling water. That's why you sit. Poor bodies, sitting there struggling day after day. It takes a few years to feel the pleasure of your physical sitting. And it is a good thing to sit while you are very young. The body is flexible.

When you get old, while sitting, even if you are "enlightened," when you see something unpleasant, you feel unpleasant. At the same time you know that feeling unpleasant is just feeling disordered. Or, when something seems too perfect, you may also feel unpleasant, because you miss disorder, which contains the beauty of life.

When your force is stabilized, you don't feel it exists, but if balance of the force is missed, you begin to feel it. Your senses have an ability to notice what's wrong. It is like recognizing a sickness which has not been diagnosed or told to you by another, but you feel it. It is an unbalanced physical condition. If it is your intestines, you discover which part of your intestines is wrong. You may feel that only the pain is sitting, just that part of your body, and the rest is all crystal, nothing there. Maybe it is your stomach sitting there, or your aching brain is sitting there. Each person has a different condition. I can look at you and see the position of your legs, where they should go, and how the position can improve your balance. You have to work slowly. Otherwise, you might say I am not your teacher, but a leg-destroyer. Not only destroying your head, but your legs, too!

These days pain is not a big problem for me. Full lotus is the best way for me to avoid pain. It is not that pain doesn't exist in full lotus, but it doesn't feel painful. Something very powerful pushes up from below.... When I undo the lotus position and start to stand up, I notice a pain. And yet, about one minute after kinhin starts, that pain goes away. (I feel so sorry talking about your pain while I don't have much pain.) When I was at Eiheiji, my legs hurt. Strangely, when I came to this country and Suzuki Roshi ordered me to "face out," the pain was gone. Maybe everybody should face out! Actually, the pain is still there, but the matter became very serious, so that eased my pain, I think. My body is getting old, and I have a little bit of crescent-moon-like pain under the kneecap. It makes me happy that there is still pain there.

For you, this practice must be very hard. I empathize with you very much. For centuries you sat in chairs, not only you, but your father, your grandfather, their grandfather, great grandfather, in Europe somewhere, all sat in chairs. Now you are asked to bend your legs. It seems impossible. I appreciate how hard it is, but it is very helpful for your zazen, so you should do it if you can. I am sorry. We, in Japan, sat on the dirt from ancient times. Now we sit on tatami mats, but it is the same as the floor. Tengai Bunryu, my natural father, taught me zazen when I was three years old. We were three children, all lined up, and he put my legs together like pizza dough. As a little child it was nothing. Without using hands I could fold up into full lotus. I can still do that. We walked around in lotus position and I still remember my father laughing at us walking and wrestling in lotus position.

You're lucky, or unlucky, to have a zabuton. In Japan only the teacher had a zabuton. The student had to sit on the tatami mat. It felt good, but certainly it was very painful. I thought at first that Eiheiji monastery was a factory of masochists and sadists, it was so painful. At Eiheiji, once you start to sit, you can never move. If you move, the elder students hit you. I don't understand it, but in one sense because I went through that period, I was able to come here to join you. That's terrible. Before I went to the monastery, I asked a couple of priests around town what practice in the monastery was like. They didn't answer, but just said, "It was fantastic! It was fantastic, afterward!"

Recently I had to translate a Japanese video film taken at Eiheiji about the monks' life there. Many of them were around twenty-two or twenty-three years old, about fifty of them. The snow was falling, very deep and beautiful, and it looked like very hard practice. It is certainly a very hard life. But once you go in and start to stretch yourself in this particular condition, you are able to live such a life. It is very strenuous. I know you experience a similar condition when you sit sesshin. Sitting still feels like disappearing from this world. You go into the rock, or the thick wall, feeling somewhat as if you are disappearing as a human being. The problem is not because of the pain in your body. The pain in the undissolved suffering in your mind remains undissolved, and yet that is what you've got. Better look at it, what it is, instead of being frightened by the appearance of it.

It's the very cold season now. It's getting up in the early morning frost, shivering, and putting on lots and lots of clothing to sit, trembling, with cold penetrating into your bones. It's slightly damp here so the coldness goes deeper. When the sun rises, a beautiful gold color, you want to fly into it instead of sitting here. You think you'll get enlightened right away! The sun is very, very wonderful, gently penetrating into you and cheering you up, brightening you up. If the sun doesn't rise because of thick clouds or fog, it helps to remember you are sitting on an enormous fire down below. The earth's surface is very cold, but down below is incredible fire, rain, and waterfalls. Our body is like that, too, so we have that kind of ability to burn in the body. Also wind goes through our nervous system all the time. The nervous system is like a perfect message channel of the god. It's called "God's channels." "Shin kei" is the Japanese word, meaning "path of the spirit."

I think Buddha was right that life is nothing but suffering. Happiness doesn't come so often. There is a story about one of Seppo's disciples whose father was a fisherman in the Yangtse River, and this young man was his helper. Every day they caught a huge carp or something in the big river. One night the moon was bright so they set up night fishing, but the father slipped and went into the water; maybe a big fish caught the hook and pulled him down. So he was drowning from the slippery river bank. The son tried to save him, and threw out his bamboo poles and fishing tackles, trying to save his father, until he, himself, was slipping, so finally he had to let the poles go. His father sank in the moonlight. The son's mind was kind of screwed up at that moment and he ran to the monastery of Seppo, "Snow Peak, Seppo Gisan," a very famous Rinzai teacher. After years of practice with Seppo, the disciple, whose name was Gensha, told Seppo, "I'm no good. I must go away from this place," so he began to climb the mountain, until, in the dark, he kicked a a sharp rock.

When he held onto his toes, they felt warm and yucky, "Oh, no, it hurts!" And he said to himself, "This body and mind do not exist, I know, but where is this pain coming from?" He sat there thinking, "Wait a minute! What did I say?" So he started to climb back down the path, back to Master Snow Peak. "I was wrong, so I came back." When the Master asked him why he had returned, he answered, "Bodhidharma hasn't come to China. The Second Patriarch hasn't gone to India." This was a strange statement since Bodhidharma came to China. Everyone knew that. And Huiko had gone to India. What he meant was that Bodhidharma didn't need to come to China and Huiko didn't need to go to India. Seppo recognized something underneath this statement, so Gensha stayed there in Kose, west of the Yangtse, and taught many people, maintaining that this entire universe is nothing but a bundle of light.

Pain is sometimes a good thing, you know.

Chapter 10

Dogen's Teaching

"What I feel now is that if you touch the core of the whole thing, you can start to study from there... You do not need to feel that you are enjoying a copy of the practice. You are doing the real practice."

Dogen's Teaching

It is very rare to be able to sit like this. People may wonder, "What's happening in that place?" Nothing! It's just people sitting, sitting, for a long time. We don't need to talk, you know. Our body has a perfect facility to receive vibrations from the next room, or that corner, or this corner. When there is some sound in the kitchen, everyone knows what happened. Even if it is a slight sound, you know, "Now that tip of carrot fell down," or something. Silence is a treasure for us now, and the receiving mind in the silent space/time is a great treasure, because we know mind is not just staying inside of this body. It goes everywhere.

We don't really need everybody to sit. Everyone is interested in their own lives and are doing what they really want to do. We are the same. You are doing this because you really want to do it. That is really good. For centuries many Japanese didn't want to do it. The thought was, "That's a monk's business!" And monasteries closed people out, operating only with the special problems of monks. My zazen teacher, Kodo Sawaki, is still criticized for encouraging people to sit, even after his death. The belief is that a secret teaching has been brought out from a deep, secret place, and if one doesn't know how valuable it is, it shouldn't be done. So a sort of hoarding of teaching is going on. But this kind of treasure cannot be seen, so there is actually no danger. The only danger is if you guide people the wrong way with it. In this sense Dogen Zenji was right that zazen practice must be studied with the right teacher, because it can take many, many years, and you can suffer with your practice, without any joy, until you finally come to understand what it has been.

Having a formulated, secret way of operating in which only devoted professionals can participate, is understandable. I studied the traditions, doing historical research, a very tiring business which I suffered with, so it should just be my suffering, and not your suffering. What I feel now is that if you touch the core of the whole thing, you can start to study from there. This is why I am here with you, to ease your minds, and tell you that knowing history, exactly how it went, is not necessary. Lack of knowledge should not make you less confident about this practice. You do not need to feel that you are enjoying a copy of the practice. You are doing the real practice. How you are is the basic point, and how you can be in the future is all up to you, not up to me. I have already given you everything I have learned in condensed form, and you are doing it. Dogen believed that the most precious jewel mankind has discovered is the opportunity to do zazen, just to do zazen and start from there. He named it the "great gate of peace and joy." Simply, it is peaceful, eternally peaceful, and pleasurable, and joyful. Because this is so, it's all up to you.

Dogen's Fukan Zazengi was written for anybody who was interested in sitting: Young or old, man or woman. We find that practice is not different for different sexes, ages, or positions. Each has his or her own way of seeking truth, but when all forms drop off from you, what remains is pure life, which you have to take care of. The most important thing is to take the best care of your own life by looking after everything around you, within you. For this big purpose age doesn't matter, for as long as your life goes on, practice goes on. Every practicer is different, and yet your individual action touches the original big purpose. That means each individual action should be done accurately, properly, and exactly. It doesn't require you to be a monk or nun, layman or laywoman, or even Buddhist or any other religious practitioner. That's my opinion.

Dogen's Advice for Sitting

Dogen Zenji says you begin by cleaning your surroundings, taking care of your daily needs, and releasing your relationships. This means you give great trust to those people's wellbeing while you are gone. Give rest and breath to myriad things. No thinking of good and bad. No judging of "yes" or "no" on anything. No trying to become a Buddha. All of this means you give up self-notion, human agency, and thinking. I always go back, year after year, after many, many sittings, and ask myself why he said those things. I thought sitting was supposed to be very simple. You just walked to the sitting place and sat on the ground and saw what happened, I used to think.

But so far, I have found the most direct and kind instruction for sitting in Fukan Zazengi. Dogen Zenji worked on this material many, many times in his life. In Fukan Zazengi it says, "Saiyu yo shin." "Sai" is "left." "Yu" is "right." "Yo shin" is "swing," like a pendulum. At the beginning of each sitting, you go from big to small "yo shin." The purpose is to find the right spot to stop. At that time it is best to close your eyes and find the center point. Do the same thing back, front, back, from your tailbone, not your waist. Your legs might not be symmetrical, but it's important to feel your body is symmetrical. Two crossed legs can never be symmetrical, because one goes on top, but by "symmetrical" I mean that your body doesn't lean one way. I am talking about balance. Feel your spine going very straight, and stretched, not piled up. It is stretched, like bamboo sections. At that time your chin naturally pulls in. When the chin goes out, immediately your mind recalls a memory. You go into the past. That's alright, but you can do it when you lie down in your bed. During sitting, you don't slip into the past. You are supposed to be in every direction and every time. It's good to sit on the ground but it is the same when you are sitting in a chair.

Dogen says, "Nose, belly in one vertical line." Strange thing to say, "Nose, belly aligned vertically. Ears, shoulder line, also vertical." "Eyes are horizontal," not tilted. "Nose is vertical." All of this makes sense to me, to let the gravity just go through you without hurting you. You come to a symmetrical position, then move out of it and feel where the center is. It may be a very slight move to find the right position of your spine. To encourage smooth breath, keep no air in the mouth. You do not want a glob of old air to stay in your mouth. Do not lean into the front or back. If you lean forward, your attention is leaning toward the future, which is not there! Leaning back, you are captured by memory. When you come to the right position you feel no thinking about future or past.

It is written in Fukan Zazengi that when you take the full lotus position, you place your right foot on your left thigh and your left foot on your right thigh. In the half-lotus, you press your left foot against your right thigh. This causes the blood current to decrease and cuts down the pain. If you keep your leg stretched, a lot of blood, and a lot of pain, goes there. The best thing is to let your skin touch the other leg. Tight pants cause more pain. When you have pain, you can try contracting your muscles so the bones come together tighter, and then release. Especially on the out breath, you let go of things. In a sense, the pain is controllable. Don't just sit there and say "Ohhh, Oohh." Contract your body, put your mind into your breath, and then with the out breath, everything goes, not just pain, but everything, goes. That controls the pain you are perceiving, preventing you from experiencing more pain.[1,2]

In finding the right position of your spine, you put your hands on your knees as you move your upper body left to right, centering your tailbone on the cushion. Your breath goes through your mouth while you are doing this rocking. Especially when you close your eyes, you can feel where the center is. When you slant or tilt one way and the other, front and back, and right and left, you can sense there is a heaviness of gravity, so you go back and forth and right and left to find the position, or your spine can start a circular motion. Then, when your hands go into the mudra, you don't feel weighted either to the left or right, front or back, so it feels like no body is there. Then you switch to nose breathing from mouth breathing. The cushion works as a wedge for your hips.

Kodo Sawaki said, "Asshole looks at heaven, peeks out at heaven." So the pelvis and back are slightly arched, and the belly is soft, round, not tight. With this belly you breathe in and out, instead of your chest opening and closing. By the movement of your belly muscles, air is going in and out through your nose. When you're stretched out in a vertical line, the tip of your nose and the bellybutton are on the same line. Your ear lobes and your shoulder line up on a vertical line.

Dogen Zenji writes: "Zazen is not learning Zen. Zazen is not practicing Zen." When you are a beginner, of ten or twenty years, you question, "Am I doing alright? Is this way the right way of practice? How about Tibetan Buddhist practice? How about other religions? Is it possible to keep my Christian belief and adopt the sitting belief?" All sorts of questions come up around this area. Every one of the teachers I studied with had a slightly different opinion, and it was very bothering. My answer to these questions is still not settled, honestly speaking, so I hope you pound your question by your practice and find answers to them by yourself. If you go crazy, before you become totally crazy, you have to talk to me about it.

Notes:

1

Sitting seiza: Seiza in Japanese means "proper sitting." It is used in Japan for formal sittings, such as the tea ceremony. Although it is probably easier if one has grown up with sitting in this position, still one can learn to sit this way and find relative comfort while meditating. It is possible to sit seiza without a pillow, kneeling, with the buttocks resting on the upturned feet, which form an anatomical cushion. Or you can use a pillow to keep the weight off your ankles. A third way of sitting seiza is to use the seiza bench, which keeps all the weight off your feet and legs and helps to keep your spine straight. These benches come in flat or tilted positions, and can be ordered with a pillow for more comfort. Sitting seiza is similar to sitting cross-legged, with straight spine, chin tucked, and hands in mudra position. ~Kate Abbe

2

Chair sitting lacks the balance and stability floor sitting provides. Although feet are in direct contact with the floor, the body seems to sit in air, so all the natural small movements of floor sitting are slightly amplified in a chair, and one moves as a blade of grass moves slightly in a small breeze. At the same time, uprightness of spine, torso, belly, lungs, breath can be identical to floor sitting. With a thin cushion under us, we sit on the edge of the chair seat, feet flat on the floor, thighs at a slight downward angle, equal weight on the sit-bones. The classical instructions to tuck the chin, align the ears, relax shoulders, are the same in either position.

Although at first, a new necessity to sit in a chair instead of a zafu can feel like a come down and a loss, knowing there is no need to stop practice when the body begins to falter, one can feel profound gratitude for a practice we can continue for a lifetime.
~Angie Boissevain

Chapter 11

Body, Mind, and Breath Sit

"...asking why we have come to this
world, and for what purpose our
existence is shaped as a human body
and mind. Trusting your own self, as
well as giving full trust to others, is
really, really hard."

Body Sits

Two days ago I said to you that you came here to sit, but that you didn't know what you were doing. I insulted you. I must take back those words. It was just me, feeling that way.

When I went to the bathroom, people were working in the kitchen and there was a person already working in the garden. And here we sit, sitting on our butts, as we say. Sitting on the cushion looks very easy, being still, like sleeping. It's an unusual thing to do, to be so still. Of course, in a sense, the body is never still, and the perceptive force of mind, the creative nature of mind, is bursting free, everywhere at once. It is not a lazy thing at all. And it is perfectly fine that you don't know what's happening to you. It wasn't an insult, so I want to take that apology back! All gods and goddesses gather to help you, without letting you know.

So, setting your head on your symmetrical sitting body, and keeping it a long time in this position, certainly promises you something is going to happen. The stillness of the physical position becomes a standard to measure things from, in a kind of creative process of understanding. When you are sitting in one position, the position of other moving things becomes clear. If both of you are moving, it is almost impossible to find out the distance moved and how your positions are changing. But you will come to understand that even if you sit in zazen for weeks and months, that stillness is relative, so leave some room for the possibility that this kind of knowledge is not definite. You may gain some confidence that you know things intuitively and comparatively, but the whole thing is still in the unknown realm. That's fine. There are many degrees of knowing. For instance, in the color red, there are many colors; in green, innumerable depths. In the same way our knowledge of things includes various depths of understanding.

I have spoken many times about posture, which is one third of the sitting position, but also the breath sits, the mind sits. It's hard to talk about zazen body and zazen mind separately. Maybe it's just a convenience to say, "From the physical, bodily perspective, I sit this way." On the other hand, one can say, "Mind alone is sitting, nothing else exists." That perspective is also possible. Also, from the viewpoint of breath, there is no body and no mind, only breath, and breath sits. You can work on these three perspectives of one sitting. But it's not like I work on my body position, my breath, and then my mind. You don't need to think that way. This point is very important in not misunderstanding sitting. You could sit your whole life with kind concerns about yourself or about the world in which you exist, and not reach to the point of sitting. Of course, bringing koan cases of any kind into zazen and working on them, is absolutely not necessary. The life you are living every moment is much more important than anything else, so you let it be free from your thoughts, from your attachments.

Mind Sits

How do you understand "mind" and "feelings"? To me, "mind" is not in my head, which represents logic, intellect, mathematics. I might say it is self, oneself, which seems to be your whole body, within and without. You might say it is you, including all of your environment. It includes people who love you, who immediately relate with you, from the past and present, all are yourself. So if I say "mind" it includes all of those. When I say, "You sit," it means mind sits, including every element of your mind, feelings, sensations. Conscious mind, which is checking your posture and breath, is something else. "Mind" is not your technique of observing your body and mind and keeping yourself together for one week.

"Mind," which we sometimes call alaya vijnana, storehouse consciousness, includes, not just the very beginning of your life, but also ancient time, which lives with you. So the person we see is small, with a long history, and a great hope for the future all included as you.

When we are practicing sitting, it looks like nothing is happening, but that is just an outlook, because there is no obvious movement or visible product, because you know lots is happening. You are recognizing, observing, your mind phenomena, playing a video of your own life story, going into a huge warehouse where everything is in disorder. Things are thrown into it, like here are some pots, some books, and there are ghost-like people. Noticing what's in there is like taking a journey into yourself, looking into your past and re-examining, reviewing all those experiences. Hakuin Zenji said zazen is to cut the main root of alaya vijnana, storehouse consciousness. You do not necessarily cut the root, but you open all doors and entrances of this storage room and let the sunlight in. It shines into the dark corners and puts things in order. Sitting is like that. It makes the wind go through and the light shine in. This is not just your own short life, this life, but it involves the roots, the previous lives of your ancestors.

A part of coming to sesshin is paying a huge debt. It's not a personal debt because we realize that we are not alone. Somebody caused a big problem and it is actually our problem, too, so in that sense, sitting alone is always sitting with the whole situation. Bodhidharma said that if you want to see a fish swimming, you have to see the water first, and if you want to catch a fish the best way is to become water and let the fish swim in it. This is what we are. You watch a fish and think that it is a fish and you are watching it, but it is all one piece.

The previous lives of our ancestors come through in our studies, helping us to know who we actually are. It is like tracing the footprints of animals or insects to tell what kind of animals they were. But we cannot stay there, in the footprints. We have to go one step ahead, because we are always one step ahead of those findings. We are tremendous manifestations, in this space, of actual living lives, constantly changing, whether we know it or not. We are always in the present, but we need to really observe what the present is, and how the past has been, to know how the future can be. That is why we are doing this.

I think some of you had sort of a hot head, today, many insights and questions, asking, "What to do with my life?" And we have this big problem of how to survive, all of us together. If we don't include all of us, it's like going to heaven with no head, or no leg. We would always have to look down and watch our partners still on earth. My master would repent every time he thought of "self and other." But we all have to do it. Otherwise, we would get stuck in Nirvana. Sitting is not living in Nirvana, it's acting from Nirvana, and seeing that each action we take affects a lot of people. It's too late to say, "I didn't mean it!" when I say something very unprepared. Many people are affected by it. So when you find you did something wrong, immediate repentance in mind and expression is necessary.

When sesshin gets so intense, on the third or fourth day, sleep becoming so shallow and short, you can call it a "heated up" state. My mind goes freely away. I say "goodbye" to sesshin and take off, running around in Paris, Tokyo, a little street in Kyoto, until Doan brings me back. "Ding dong, ding dong!" I rush back. What I was dreaming about seemed more real than actually being there. These experiences make me wonder what this mind is. It must be like an electric molecule. If someone in Japan turns the switch, they receive my message immediately. Your thought pattern is with someone, and the one who receives it may be another person who is thinking about you at the same time you are thinking about them, and you have a conversation. You don't know whether it happened or not, but later you find out it happened so you feel very mystified. I speak here in a small voice, but actually it is from the other end of the earth you can hear it.

A dream is not just a dream, it's a recognition in sleep, similar to your mechanism of thinking in wide-awake time, so a piece of a dream recalled when you are awake is a part of your thought. It's like wind came in the night and a leaf fell. In the morning you pick it up and see, "Oh, that's a piece of my dream." Also, day dreams, themselves, are fantastic creations. We spend a lot of time creating them, and how you evaluate them is up to you. You may understand them or make sense of them as you would a dream. It's up to you. If I said you were doing fantastically, and you said you agreed, even though you didn't feel that way, you would never meet who you want to meet. Who you want to see, truly, is actually your own self.

Do you realize the change of your mind-condition during sesshin? What do you think the difference is between mind in regular life and mind in sesshin? Everybody knows the answer. Your mind responds to the surrounding circumstances, so the more information that is coming in, the more activated the mind is. During sitting, kinhin, standing, in sesshin the mind expands, responding to the many, many, many things around you. Even the sleep pattern changes in sesshin. The last few days people didn't sleep much. It's kind of resting, with a very deep short sleep. Still, your mind was awake during that sleep. You noticed every single sound, and yet, your mind was completely resting. I think the moon is really full these days, and your body feels it, even through the ocean fog which covered this place last night.

What kind of sitting mind is with you? Sometimes, the mind sits still. Sometimes it freezes colder than ice. Sometimes it boils more than hot water. So we observe the quality of our life and directly, kindly, deal with it, wisely relate with it. It's your life, nobody else's, so you are in charge of taking care of it. Nobody controls your life.

When you introduce others to meditation, how to properly sit, you usually give instructions for the body, physical instructions directed toward a meditative position. You don't mention so much about how the mind meditates, how the mind sits. But, obviously, that is a very big concern for people who want to meditate. We say, "taming the body," "taming the mind," and "tuning the breath." As you see, these three aspects or ways of approaching meditation are because you were born as a human being with body, mind, and breath. Each of these is an approach to what you are, how life is manifested, a way of picking up the bodily condition of your whole being. What do you mean by "body"? Do you limit your own being by the skin border or the energy field of your bodily being, or do you include as far as your mind can reach? Understanding of bodily existence varies, accordingly.

Breath Sits

Certainly, sitting like this in zazen is a very unusual thing for human beings to do. Here is a very, very enormous, heavy head sitting on your shoulders, and a very flexible, serpent-like body, spine, and bones. When you move around and stretch your spine, your whole body feels different. All of a sudden a channel of breathing opens up, so air can go straight. I have said that if you open your chest too much it is very difficult to breathe, so your ear and your shoulder should be in the same vertical line. As Dogen said, the tip of your nose and belly button are in a vertical line. How far you pull in your chin affects your ability to breathe, so you have to find the best position for your chin. If it is pulled in too much, it is impossible to breathe.

One important thing to mention again is that no air should remain in your mouth while you breathe through your nose. Do you understand that? You should have no air inside of your mouth, no space for old air to stay. It seems that when air is in your mouth, more bubbles of thoughts come into your mind. To keep the air out of our mouth we have "zazen lips." There is a slight tension at the ends of your lips, and they go slightly up and make a smiling face. Smiling lips, so to speak. Try. And then, expand your tongue, touching the upper dome, and the tip of your tongue goes behind the teeth, and touches from behind.

The breath comes and goes, like a swinging door, a very fine swinging door that the wind pushes in and pushes out. You cannot tell which is the in-breath, which is the out-breath. Hakuin Zenji mentioned that, for smooth breath, you put a down feather underneath the "waterbird" here (below nostrils). It doesn't move. The air goes in and out, but the feather doesn't move. The air doesn't make a sound, and long breath goes long; shallow breath goes shallow. No one notices that you are breathing. That kind of breath is zazen breath. I learned breathing from butterflies. One day I was sitting at Tassajara, and I felt in tune with the breath of everything. The trees were breathing. About twenty butterflies were sitting on hot rocks, very white hot rocks, with clean water cascading between them. The butterflies were all breathing at once, opening their wings, and I tuned them in. It was very fantastic to feel that.

Where does breathing originate, what is the beginning and end of each in-breath, out-breath? Who, or what, is breathing?

And in the breath are two other elements, the bodily element and the mind element. When you pick up the mind quality of your being, things are much more complicated because of the depth of the invisible mind. We don't know who is breathing. It looks like you are breathing. The body says the body is breathing. Is the mind breathing? Air going in and being cast out is the noticeable, physical, part of breath. Yet, prana is life force which is neither coming out of you, nor coming in from outside. It is the breath of the universe, so to speak. When the first flower blooms in the spring, it shows winter is over and spring has come. But what is blooming is not just the flower, everything is blooming. Our life is like that. Each of our lives is like that. The whole world is involved in each person's existence.

When you breathe, it feels like you are doing it, but, actually, the whole universe is breathing each breath with you.

So when you do not make a special effort, but let the breath be, let it breathe as your body responds, you feel perfect. I especially feel the mystery of the in-breath, and the letting go of personal concerns with each out-breath. That's what I'm very much interested in these days. What comes in is absolutely new life, recovery of your new life, new chance, new thoughts. I went down to the lake today and saw a big blue heron fluttering. It had huge wings. I went down a little farther and saw many shoots of water grass. It felt good to see that new, powerful life coming back.

Continuously I suggest that you have good posture, because posture is a sort of proof of the mind situation, a reflection of your invisible life which penetrates the body. Let your mind ride on good breathing, smooth, deep, even breathing, coming in and going out, which keeps you from slipping out of the present moment. As soon as you forget the breath, mind phenomena color your breath and all sorts of movies go on in that breath. Your body continuously reflects whatever is going on in those personal movies. We like to let them go and forget them, or maybe finish them, but I don't want to say you should just forget them. The one who keeps watching, keeps letting the whole thing happen, is a very important part of yourself. This is not necessarily a judging function, just an observing one.

Chapter 12

Different Practices

"Is zazen the method or the purpose?"

Contemplation

There are many contemplative practices: Moonlight sitting, sunlight sitting, snow sitting, rain sitting. Whatever nature's condition is, you sit in it and find out both what it is and what is yourself. You find out how it is to live in those conditions. Counting breath is also one technique, especially recommended for a busy-minded state, when your mind cannot stop jumping from one thing to another. It's probably a chemical imbalance. In this state you can't relax in the present moment because this computer mind goes on and on, and your emotions change from one to another.

Vipassana and Shamatha

Before he began practicing tapas Shakyamuni Buddha received teaching from two sages, Uddaka Ramaputta, and also Alara Kalama. They were teaching *Vipassana*, or *Shamatha*. Vipassana usually is called "insight meditation." *Vi*, in Sanskrit, means precise division, specific knowledge, exactly what is. *Pass* is to perceive. Since Sanskrit is a mother language of English, you can understand this rather easily. Vipassana is concerned with the sense organs: Eyes, ears, nose, tongue, body. Sixth is mind, or consciousness, seventh is stained, habituated consciousness, or *klista manas*. Eighth is alaya vijnana. Alaya means to store. All your consciousness, all your past and present experiences and information, are stored. Most of our *alaya* vijnana is in a messed up state. We don't know what is where.

Vipassana is not an analytical study of our mind function, but rather a theoretical division of our mind. The first seven divisions are like visualizing your own experiential mind consciousness. The seventh consciousness, klista manas, functions when you smell something, like incense, or the fragrance of a flower. Immediately you feel good and say, "I like it." Or when you smell something burning, cloth burning, or gas half-burned, you don't like it. This like-dislike is what the seventh consciousness is conducting. It also includes like-unlike. Sometimes you meet with people and feel immediate familiarity. When you meet with an orangutang in the zoo, you think, "That's my family, but I'm not like that!" You are very much alike but you deny your identity. This is the realm of klista manas which makes exact differentiation. You can understand how it developed through the establishment of human society.

The eighth consciousness, alaya vijnana, includes all existences as your own self. This includes mountains, trees, clouds, whatever you experience. Although you still retain your individuality among all existences, when you are in alaya vijnana, you have no words to say "I and thou, I and you, I and that," or "they, he or she." It is all "I," so to speak. This "alaya vijnana" is a rather fundamental, universal consciousness which we all depend on. It is a somewhat theological concept, which relates to Vipassana and Shamatha meditation. "Vipassana, Shamatha", are two vocabulary words which are actually inseparable, like mind and body are inseparable. Yet, from the mind side, there is no body, and from the body side there is no mind. But we were born to see our existence from both aspects, and the two adjoin and make sense. So if you say, "I am a pure materialist," you are saying there is only matter in this world. If you say, "There is no matter, every existence is nothing but a manifestation of mind," that is also a possible perspective. However, if you rely upon only one aspect, you always have a problem. This conversation has been an endless debate among humans, and the philosophical settlement is still unresolved.

Listen to the creek. You stop hearing it when I am talking but the creek becomes loud when your mind is in the state of shamatha, a deep degree of shamatha. Vipassana, insight, perseverance, increases. You have memories relating to the sound. You can imagine what kind of creek it is. Not a huge waterfall, it's a tiny creek, running here and there hitting rocks. You see a long, long pattern of the creek. With every objective image which comes to you, your shamatha and vipassana are always working together. As a process of establishing your meditative function, with vipassana you go in. Your concentrated mind stays on each object, one at a time, for some length of time. You observe the flame of a fire, not only how it burns and moves, but memories of your life from ancient time comes back to you. You see reflections of the sun, sometimes direct sunlight, or you stare at the light of a sunset, and many insights come to you, as if the sun is talking to you as your mother or your father, as life-giver to you. Especially when you experience the warming moments in the sunrise, your body starts to understand the relationship of your body and sunlight. At the moment of the sunrise or sunset, light penetrates into your body at the "third eye." While listening to the water, when you face each other in the sangha, what that water, various sounds of running water, brings to you, is understanding of each other, going very deep.

The moon, which arises and sets, reflects many, many states of existence. Moon contemplation, we call it. Practically every object can become the subject of your contemplation by vipassana. Needless to say, this is just an explanation of how your mind has been working from your birth day until today. Nobody has taught you, but if you recall how your meditative, contemplative, concentrative activity goes back to your childhood, you understand. I know something made you stop and listen and taste, and especially, see. Surprisingly, you already experienced innumerable vipassana from your birth day. Every activity we are engaging in, devoting ourselves to, deeply interested in, has this nature of vipassana: Insight, knowing, awakening, and unfolding. Phenomena unfold the teaching in front of you, within you. At that time, you realize your perceptive faculty is in deep shamatha, balanced, still, ready to receive, or act.

Shamatha is bodily stillness, mind stillness. Your body and mind are a round mirror on your cushion. If it moves around, the world moves with it. In shamatha you define yourself as, so to speak, nothing, a knowing system, to go back to when the world was born, when you were born. The world has been with you ever since as the exact identity with yourself and you have been existing in the center of it. At some point we discovered our process-consciousness as "I," as "Kobun," as each of you, and it started to separate from what you were, up to that time. Then, naturally, you started to create knowlege with which you could properly communicate with other existences. Thus language became a necessary vehicle to communicate with other people, in order to understand them. It's a highly complicated existence we have. What I want to say is, there is nobody else to destroy as your enemy, as your fearful enemy.

Koans

Several people practice with teachers who encourage constantly practicing with koans, not just during sitting, but entire days, day and night. On the other hand, there are people, like, most of the time, myself, who don't talk about koans, who disagree with the use of koans, especially during sitting. We say those people are in the Soto tradition. But it is not quite true. There are many teachers in the Soto school who pound their practice personally by studying koans and other historical wisdom. They study not only Chinese koans, but koans in every sense. When you read something and ask, "What does this mean?" this question opens you up. In the Bible, the Koran, the Torah, are a lot of stories, and in the biographies of saints and sages you have various kinds of koan subjects.

It seems that all koans are related to the basic pattern of one's self-realization. The relative self is related to the absolute presence. It is a constant interest. In your innermost place this meeting with the Absolute is the essential subject. When you succeed in it, at that moment you feel your life is perfect. It's supposed to be perfect. But it doesn't, of course, continue its perfection moment after moment. Even the teachers of koans say, "You passed this koan. Next, you work on this one." There are some very strange koans. My elder brother, Hojosama, trained me in various koans and made me cry, literally, because he is my elder brother, so when I failed I went after him with my fist!

One koan he gave me was this: "Imagine you have completed digging a deep hole in the ground." And I said, "Yes, I dug it, deep. No one can climb up from the bottom. I did it, now what do you want?" "Now you go get a national treasure from the shrine, Shakyamuni Buddha's statue." "Yes, I have carried it." "Now you set it right here at the edge of the hole. You sit here. Choose one to go. You, or this treasure. Choose one." I was a very obedient young Buddhist at that time. Very young. Of course, I put the Buddha here on the bank and I jumped in the hole. He said, "Uh, uh!" And then we wrestled for one hour. Such a simple koan. Then he said, "Yes, that is very true." I passed it.

Then my brother said, "That's not all. Let's go to the garden." We had a lotus pond our father built, a big lotus pond, about the size of the pond here, only the shape is different. Many koi are in there. "Now," he says, "let's sit down." There was a very big stepping stone at the end of the hopping stone, right there by the bank. We look in the water, and here comes a huge, very big koi, going back and forth. "You see that?" "Yes, I see." "Right now, right this second, catch it without making your hand wet!" It took about one week. Every day he said, "Got it?" Finally I recalled if you want to know the mind of the fish, you've got to know the mind of the water. This is a famous word of Bodhidharma. That word clicked in my head and the next day I told him,

"I got it!" And I touched my hand on the ground like this, "Right now I caught it." And he said, "Mm. Yes." "That fish is in the water, and then I caught the water with this. How about this!" And he said, "Pretty good."

I don't know where he got those koans. Such fragrant stories flower from an earnest practice. We all know those koan stories, and various doctrinal teachings in Buddhist history. There is nothing wrong with studying all of them if you want to. They are so rich, if you go through one after another, find where the story came from, which part of the world these people lived in, what kind of people were exchanging this dialog. It makes you feel like you are creating a scenario for the theatre. By putting the theatre together and looking at it, or even playing part of it, you start to understand where this happened, how this happened and why it was brought up.

Of course, in my way of relating to you, I do not encourage you to work on Soto koans during zazen. Sitting should be utterly open. It's an utter gift, so it shouldn't have a price tag, or any intention involved in it. That's how I see it. But in the realm of encounter, not with your own self but in relationship, perhaps at the beginning of being noticed by someone as a student, because your deep admiration for them is realized, this koan subject is quite important. The koan is a skillful means of facing someone behind the koan, the living entity. Here at the other end of the koan is another big living entity. The two living things face each other and the koan begins to arrive. Most koan subjects appear as a spark of light in the meeting of people. Do you remember Hyakujo and the nose twisting? Wild geese were flying from the reed as two monks were walking. It's rude to twist someone's nose without permission, but the koan subject was very important. One said, "Oh, the geese flew away." "Ouch!" was the next thing he said. The friend who walked with him said, "That's not true!" Of course he didn't say that, but just twisted his nose. "The geese didn't fly away. The geese are right here. Maybe there is a scale upon your eyes. Take your glasses off so you can see things more clearly."

In the Rinzai lineage and the Soto lineage are different ways to relate to zazen, or different ways to relate to the person. The zazen, itself, might be the same. It's like one school teacher gives homework to the student and the student comes back with the homework done. Another teacher doesn't give any homework and the student still comes back. There is an advantage and disadvantage in each case. When I think about koans, I cannot breathe. My head goes shwew! I totally forget the koan, and enjoy breathing. That's my habit when someone gives me a koan, like my brother. No peaceful sitting.

The disadvantage of no koan is sleeping in the sleep. That's very bad. You go through various stages of sleep. You pick up a new-fallen leaf from the pond and you go on and on like that, picking up one, another one, and another one. Visions of your latest experience come to you, and then come many related experiences in your past. They all come back, and then you don't know what's coming next. In the end, it's very exhausting. You start to space out. The subconscious field of the brain is such a fantastic storage, anything can come out from it.

Soto Zen

Is zazen the method or the purpose? This is an important subject. The method and the actual achievement are different. This is why different practice lineages occurred. Emphasis on wisdom through koan practice is one current, the Rinzai lineage, which became very powerful a few generations after the Sixth Patriarch. Another is the Soto lineage, of Sozan-Tozan, named for Tozan, who lived about the same time as Rinzai, and Sozan, his student. There are many other lineages. When you look into each lineage holder and their biographies, you find many teachings condensed in each teacher.

I have been taught in the Soto tradition, but the more I know of what Soto tradition means, the less sense it makes to say "Soto," although I am interested in talking about what kind of zazen this name, "Soto," points toward. It was two persons' names, disciples of the Sixth Patriarch, put together, but it also refers to Sokei Zan, the Sixth Patriarch's sangha. "Zan" is "mountain," referring to an actual mountain and to the shape and feeling of mountain. It is this feeling, when you face a mountain, causing an incredible sensation in your body, which is why the Sixth Patriarch's sangha was named "Sokei Zan."

So I'd like to reveal to you how natural the experience of sitting fully really is, but if I put my own concept on it, making you understand that how I think is the ideal way to sit, then I would be a gardener who makes boxes and lets you grow through them and become square bamboo. I say you cannot call this "Zen" or "Buddhism," but I also want you to know there is a great danger in the unidentified way, too. People ask, "Then, what are you?" To have no identification is so insecure, in one sense. Some people really feel it isn't good, or it isn't how it should be. But, as you notice, no one forced you or ordered you to do this, so my great hope is for your success, in a real sense, from the practice you do in this sesshin.

Shikantaza

Even if you pile up hundreds of text books of all kinds, alas, unless you have the eye which perceives the author's soul through the words, you never reach the point. You just hear and read and take in as much as you are able to understand, and that's all. For example, a text may say, "When you do plain sitting, just sit without any contemplation on any teachings. Set all teachings aside and become just a bare person. The myriad things concerning you, set them aside, and sit. Even the effort to become Buddha, you set aside." But we want to bring all of these things into the sitting. After we sit for a while, all of those fancy pieces of junk are going to shine. That's what we want. So you sit and sit and sit with hot blood full in your head. All kinds of memories, impressions, perceptions, knowledge, theories, ideas, doctrines, without thinking, you see through. It is very strict guidance, given in order to reveal your own truth, your own life-dynamic, undefeatable, and so fragile, so uncertain. You dig out your life dynamic, as it is, and place it on the cushion. That is an extremely kind instruction for zazen.

There is a difference between the shikantaza way and the way of many other sitting meditations. I feel it more and more clearly. It is not about the contents of each sitting, but the attitude with which you sit, and how your sitting appears. Utter trust in your sitting appears as the continuous effort of keeping the finest posture you can make. Sometimes we fall into various spaces where there is drowsiness, darkness, thinking. The body condition is not always stable so we sink into various places even though we are making utter effort to sit straight. Some periods are very hard and we move a lot. Others are no difficulty. You sense your body on the surface, a little under the surface, and also deep inside, in all parts. By saying, "shikantaza" we imagine there is some special stage, psychological, physical, or spiritual, that we experience. That's how we tend to think. But "shikantaza," the word itself, points to action. The purest form of sitting action is called "shikanta." "Za" means sitting. "Purest" means anybody can do it, old, young, man, woman. People who believe in different religions, spiritual traditions, without changing their belief, still can do it. I say "purest" but "plain" is what I mean. Before religion began, before Buddhism came about as a historical order and cultural phenomenon, sitting was already there. Unstained. Shikantaza isn't the name of a religion, but it is a very religious way to live.

I know you have gone through many phases of believing in this form of sitting, then doubting it. You wonder to yourself, instead of sitting so formally, so intensely, why don't you just be comfortable, on the sofa, coffee cup and your favorite text book next to you, and think about being still and observing your life-dynamic? Why do we have to sit so hard? No coffee! No book! No phone! It's like a person who was caught and put in jail. Self-caught jail!

Chapter 13

Forgetting the Self

"When you see a bird you become the bird. Do you know that? Just seeing it is becoming it. If it were otherwise, this ability of seeing or listening would not be given to us. If you like a great big snow mountain, you become that. Dogen left very beautiful words on that high, distant mountain, "The mountain belongs to who loves it most.""

Forgetting the Self

One period of sitting is not your own sitting. You may feel it is your sitting, but the inner view, which is utterly the external view as well, is that your personal existence is not sitting, but is included in sitting. The inner view includes everything which your mind is continuously working on. Memories arise. Memories of your experiences are always there, no matter whether you deny them or accept them. They are there. Moreover, time passes, contents change, and so posture allows you to keep going. As you notice, this physical existence is very dynamic, a living thing which you cannot stop because it goes by itself. Maybe the contents are living things, who go by themselves, and you are that which is experiencing and feeling them.

Why do we forget the self? To attain supreme perfect enlightenment? I am sorry, it isn't so. Facing the wall means to shoulder the world and forget yourself. Maybe we'd better not think of this action too much. It is a kind of discovered wisdom, like our posture and breathing. Each of us discovers our best way. We drop all kinds of preconceptions of what we are, what we have been, what we wish to be, or will be. We give those thoughts about ourselves a rest. You eventually go back, but you do not stick on the habitual way of knowing yourself, rather, you let yourself be free to see yourself among all things. In Fukan Zazenji, Dogen said, "Set all those myriad concerns aside when you plunge into sitting." Like a person who is about to go for a swim, you forget about what kind of clothing you are wearing. Just take them all off and jump into the water. Some people may go into the water with a newly bought dress! It is not necessary to bring it into zazen. A billion dollars doesn't help much, either, in fact it rather hinders your ability to be free from all kinds of agency. This is an opportunity to give yourself total freedom to discover at what time something is going to happen and what kind of manifestation will take place. Once mind is concentrated, as you all know, it creates something. So direct it in the best conditions, place, and time. This is important.

"No-self" is not a doctrine, it simply describes how things are. If truth is truth, it is true for everybody. Anatman is the Indian terminology. Anatman is something to do with Brahman and Atman, God and a person. This term, "anatman", was a denial of the Indian view of the personal relationship of Atman as your self, with God at the other end of it. It meant "not-self." In China the same subject was discussed using the word, "mu," emptiness, not in the ontological sense of existing or not existing. If someone faces you and says, "You look like you exist, but actually you don't exist," that's very insulting to you. Yet, sometimes, as a stage of self realization, one can say, "'I' don't exist." On a metaphysical level you both exist and don't exist. As your own recognition, "no-self" is one kind of observation you have reached. It doesn't need to be true forever. It is just one understanding about your self-being. The famous koan, Joshu's "mu," is not just a Zen story. It is everybody's story. Sometimes the answer to whether there is Buddha nature in oneself, was "yes," sometimes it was "no." In Japan we take this same subject in a not so serious way, I think. The closest word I can use is "as if," "as if" something exists. You want to be truly close to the truth, but if you say, "This is true," you are finished. I mean, you fall into the biggest pit and you never come out. So you say, "It is as if..."

When you see a statue of Saint Mary holding her baby, it doesn't matter if you are a man or woman. After you observe it for awhile, you become it and then you know what you are holding. And if you see someone dancing, when you really feel that is a fantastic dance, actually you are dancing that dance. So the very important point here is that in order to form the sitting posture as you wish it, you create it. It is not only that which was taught to you, but it results from a somewhat deep wish to be in the meditative space. "Nothing" carried you to this posture, which is a chance to be alone in a pure sense, and it is ultimately simple. Carried by this "nothing" you reach an understanding that everything is what you are.

When you see a bird you become the bird. Do you know that? Just seeing it is becoming it. If it were otherwise, this ability of seeing or listening would not be given to us. If you like a great big snow mountain, you become that. Dogen left very beautiful words on that high, distant mountain, "The mountain belongs to who loves it most."

Our language, which was transmitted to us from very long ago up to today, is also a very important treasure. Because of language, our sense organs taste, see, not necessarily things as they are, but as they are supposed to be seen and tasted. Your immediate sensing of the words you hear and the words you understand, are also an ability you were given. Maybe we trained ourselves somewhat, but the ability, itself, was already embedded in our life. Thinking of these things, I have been feeling that nothing is made by me. Everything belongs to the world, including from the very center of my being. This body belongs to all. I am here, but it doesn't belong to me.

Sambogha Samadhi

Once in a while you sense your entire being is in utter samadhi. It's a state of forgetting your own self, as if the "self" of yourself does not exist as you thought it existed. Some great dynamic, gigantic life is manifesting its own course and you don't know who you are or where you are located. It doesn't matter any more. Something is going on, and that something has clearly achieved itself as what it is. Any kind of samadhi has this awareness of being as something. When someone is totally involved in one action, such as reading, or writing, or planting, building, speaking, the action is called samadhi. Samadhi is opposite to the state of mind which is scattering, moment after moment, capturing different objects, not settling down to its own well-balanced function. You might called it confused, or unfocused, when seeing is not focused, listening is not focused, so you cannot achieve the right perception. Most of the time we are in this state, with too many interesting objects out there, which are actually projected within, and stimulated mind is continuing to reflect the external changes which interest you.

Zazen can be called Sambhoga samadhi. You return and melt into it when you sit. Actually it is Dharmakaya, Sambhogakaya, Nirmanakaya, all three bodies of Buddha. They are always one. You cannot divide them. You realize that you are going into sitting, through your breathing, when you come into the sitting room. When breath is aware, tamed, your mind is already sitting. It's like Pavlov's dog who begins to salivate when he hears the bell. Our breath is like that. You are calling your breath back.

Sambhoga means to accept and let it function. When you receive food, food becomes your life force. When you take water, the glass of water satisfies your thirst and the thickness of your blood and other fluids in your body become kind of loosened. There is scientific understanding of what elements come in with the in-breath, what they do, and what goes out with the out-breath. Some energy, some movement is created when you breathe in, or when you eat food. What you do, how you manifest the energy, in turn determines what happens to you. So simply imagining or thinking of meditation doesn't fulfill our practice. Actually doing it confirms in time/space what is happening to you even though the whole figure of what happens is not necessarily understood.

Competition and Compassion

Usually our mind does not care about other people. With a competitive mind, if somebody dies, you'll think, "Oh, good, I have more to eat." Or if somebody falls in a race, you think, "See, I am stronger!" That is how our mind works. Yet competitive mind and compassionate mind both have the same root. How do they differ? If somebody you love more than yourself falls, you cannot say, "Oh good!" Instead, you think you are dead, that you, yourself, have fallen down. It is really a very slight difference. Bodhidharma's Ninth Precept, "No indulging in anger," means that the moment you give birth to self, the small "I," all of a sudden "many" becomes "others." "Many" means everyone is yourself, but as soon as you realize there is "I," all who were yourself become "others." Keeping this attitude moment after moment is very intense anger toward the very minor sorrow of separation. Separation, intense loneliness, causes enormous anger. Because of the self clinging of this being when it grows, anger grows. This occurs when people are being concerned about themselves, as themselves. When you raise illusory self and attach to it moment after moment, you become alone, of course. Separation is like that. The departure of yourself from others is like that.

Where is the division of you and other things? Is skin the division of you and others? I don't think so. Air, big air and little air in you, is a good example. As you breathe in, where is the limitation? The concept of Brahman and Atman in Hindu tradition is the same. The Godhead, God, and yourself is one piece of existence. All that exists is God and you, and others are another part of you, so to speak. In Chandugya Upanishad it says, "In the center of your heart is the pavilion of God." That is, God dwells in you and God is impossible to measure, what it is, who it is, what it is doing to you. To some extent the life of you and God is simultaneous. It goes together as one thing. The more we think about this kind of strange condition we've got, the more mystified we feel. The real reason why you were born and why or how your mind/body is working like this on this earth, that's a very big question.

Dogen mentions somewhere in Shobogenzo that we are lucky to have this human life, although it is swift as morning dew. So keep every moment as a treasure to do something with it. Congratulations to you. Each of your antenna, your way-mind, is so polished. Full intelligence, and somewhat good health, brought you here. We have this rare opportunity to sit together.

Chapter 14

Thoughts on Kensho, Faith, Life, Love and Death

"Kensho and samadhi are temporary. You cannot dwell in them. If you dwell in them, they become the most powerful Mara."

Kensho

You relive, over and over again, something that sank into your subconscious, and is newly revealed in sitting. At work, or at home, you experience it again and again. It's like taking hundreds of photographs in your body. Each of these points of awareness is like a shutter opening and closing. You take the picture and it sinks into your subconscious feelings. Maybe one or two shots are especially impressive to you, sometimes fearful, sometimes joyful. It is like undeveloped film in your closet. When we come to sesshin and sit many times a day, all those are developed. The relationships of these perceptions become clear. We call this pratitya samutpada, "co-depending origination." You see the relationship of all things, from past to future, from high to low. You are able to look at things in all directions, in different dimensions. And your existence is part of it, your own perseverance is part of it. During sitting time this truth of how things are existing and how you are existing as a person in this world is revealed more and more clearly to you. If you push against the movement, the direction of how things are existing, you have pain. If you flow with the movement, you feel freedom. You don't get out of it, rather, you flow with it and have a sensation of freedom. It doesn't mean freedom to go off somewhere. So in your sitting, how much or how little you want to look at is up to you. I cannot do anything about it. And I also don't want to talk about it unless you want to talk about it, because it's gone. When you start to talk about it, it becomes a spoken thing, an already experienced thing.

"Kensho" or "Gensho" is perceiving, realizing, true nature. "Ken" means "perceive," "sho" is the nature of things. These two words, "kensho" and "gensho" are actually the same thing, actualization. When you see the true nature, your appearance shows it. Your presence is seen as one who realized Buddha nature, so to speak. So the teacher doesn't need to talk, just look, and you, yourself, also know it. You can express it in any way, any way which shows the realization of Buddha nature.

We do not talk about kensho so much in our practice. How to nourish, how to continue and generate your life many more times in this practice, is our concern. Kensho does not happen just once. A thousand times you realize it and expand. This is nothing new I'm talking about. Your growth, your interest in daily life, doing things for yourself and others, all relate to this polishing out of true nature as it wants to be polished out, brightened, strengthened, sometimes healed, so that it recovers its original power.

Kensho and samadhi are temporary. You cannot dwell in them. If you dwell in them, they become the most powerful Mara. No one can relate with you. Hopefully, some blockage dissolves, something opens up and you can move on. Whatever the cause of your opening-up experience, you cannot repeat it. You can remember, of course, but you cannot repeat the same experience again. This tells you, you have to wipe out all such experiences and not idealize them. You release your experience, which is called practice after enlightenment. It may have an amazing effect on you, ecstatic joy or sometimes incredible pain, but when the period of sensation ends, it ends. Every one of us is like that, we act different each time. Maybe one wrinkle of the brain opens, and we become a little bit wiser. We should all grow up and be enlightened, and then say goodbye! Dogen said, "Mind/body dropped off." We don't know what he meant. Intellectually, we can suspect what feeling it was, but it must have been a very big occasion to Dogen. Each person has a different way to express a kensho experience. You must remember several such occasions in your life.

I have said that kensho means "perceiving," or "realization." We say, "original face appears," not just as a human being, but as a total being. Sometimes our imagination creates experiences like "satori," which means "mind-easy." It's not very special, in fact, it's very ordinary, and sometimes it's untrue. Or I could say that it's a little part of the cosmic reality, so it's not untrue. At some point before each of us was created, we started to decrease our imagination, but satori requires a gigantic imagination! I have had some satori experiences, but I always ask myself, "Was that it?" I do know it is always happening, but usually our conscious mind and senses cannot capture it. Occasionally you go very close to satori and still a question mark remains. It is the essence of life, but if we cling to it, our heart will stop immediately. The miraculous state of our body and mind, we know, but we don't see the way each cell is actually vibrating and manifesting. We only feel something warm, so we conclude our body must be burning light.

You have to let go of those ecstatic states, ecstatic pits. You experience them, and keep going. It is said we can count fifty-three kinds of "makyo," which are delusions, formed according to our sense organs and our circumstances, our internal and external conditions. It is something like when you are climbing a mountain, and you reach a peak; seeing no more rocks to climb, you feel fantastic. You put a sign, a rock, on the peak, "So and so arrived here." All of a sudden a strong wind comes up, the clouds are blowing away, and you look around at the high, snowy peaks which are revealed around you. You have to say, "Oh, this wasn't the peak. It was just the top of one of the lower hills." Makyo is like that. We can easily sit down and relax and feel, "This is it!" It might be an accomplishmnent, an achievement of any kind, maybe a kensho experience. Hakuin Zenji talks about this. When he was about fifty-four years old, after various kensho experiences, satori experiences, he came again to Tozan Zenji's koan, "Go i," "Five Stages of Practice." He confessed, "I have experienced innumerable little satori, and earlier I thought I understood Tozan Zenji's koan completely. But today I see I didn't understand Tozan Zenji." The first kensho Hakuin Zenji experienced was listening to the distant temple gong and his mind opened. Another time he was listening to the autumn crickets. That kind of experience happened innumerable times, he said. So he made a new Bodhisattva out of Hell, "Homage to the Bodhisattva of Great Hell." Such a strange, strange person he was.

When you sit down in any stage of achievement and quit making an effort to go on and on, even if that was a fantastic awakening to you, it becomes a hindrance. Like tonight's sushi was great, but the taste is gone. We don't cling to the experience.

Our Faith

In the Biblical tradition there is the teaching that the created one finally goes back to the creator, and faith is the only path to it. Isn't this so? By finding out what is the will of the creator, and putting every effort into doing what the creator wishes you to do, then this linkage is accomplished. We all know about this, that the creator is the origin and the created one has some identity with the creator, but the created one cannot take the place of the creator. This is one example of the way I understand the logic of the Judeo-Christian tradition, their logic of how faith takes place.

We can talk about faith and trust between people because of this basic pattern of the creator and the created. In other words, when you see a creator behind a person or things, your faith pierces through whomever you are relating to, to the creator. Then faith is accomplished. In the same manner, when I think about how to relate with people and things, it has to do with something which is eternal in a limited existence. You project your eternity to the eternity behind others. A monk came to Joshu and asked, "This dog, does he have Buddha nature?" Joshu answered, "Yes, Buddha nature." Another monk asked the same question and he said, "No, no Buddha nature." It's confusing. The words, "Buddha nature" themselves are a very big problem. Can you say what is the nature of Buddha? It is a Sanskrit word which is the mother language of your own English language, so you must know better than me. If I say "Buddha nature," "Busho," as a Japanese, it is a very confusing word.

What are the roots of "Buddha, Dharma, Sangha"? They are your mother language. You have to study them more. To me they are a completely foreign language. We say Buddha is the "enlightened one." Metaphorically, we understand this, when darkness subsides and things appear clearly in your mind's eye, in your fresh eye, you perceive your position, what confronts you, what exists in your awareness in the relationship between your self and others. You see how things actually exist and relate. You see what brought you together and what's in you, between you and others. This is the perseverance of the Dharma, the precise, excellent Dharma, which is ultimate and unchangeable. You see the law of all existence, the truth of all existences, as they are, as they are able to exist. That is what Dharma is.

The most important thing is Annutara-samyaksambodhi. The expansion of universal truth you have observed feels like a discovery you are making. Seeking your own truth, you end up viewing the truth of the universe within which you live. And yet this truth you have been viewing is not changed by your discovery. You are seeing a partial view of what truth was, or has been. Even if we stretch our capacity to the ultimate, the limitation of the knowing function of this body and mind is so limited, so self-centered, that you feel your knowledge does not reach to the edge of truth itself. Although your mind completely identifies itself with the unchangeable truth, itself, still, it is a very helpless recognition.

Life and Death

Is life going to continue even after death? You use the words, "pass on." Sounds great! You pass on and on, hopefully. But we actually don't know what happens when this body falls off, like a ripe persimmon, or a heavy blossom which cannot stay any more, and falls on the ground to deteriorate and become soil, and gas, and return to its elements. Even so, we still want something to remain there. Don't you? You do. And something pops out from that persimmon, or fallen blossom, and goes into something, again. If it is a ripe persimmon, the next generation has been prepared in it. Most plants are like that. And in our life, raising a family is like that. But once in a while you really face your aloneness, and the knowledge that we will pass on alone without knowing what will happen after that. We wish so much that the next life will be better! Some people say, "This life was the last one. Such a yucky life. I don't want it any more."

We constantly pass away and constantly recover from death, so that, while we don't call it "life and death" each breath is new, and each breath is separate. You don't put a number on it. It is only one breath, and when one breath is done, that's all. Our moment of life is like that. You really taste the beginning of inhalation, the end of inhalation, the beginning of exhalation. During exhalation, especially at the end of exhalation, you observe what's in it. Your body tells you what it is, and mind can appreciate what it is. In other words, at the end of exhalation, you stop breathing. You stop until you scream for life. Not sensing just the breath in your nose, you really taste, you really understand, what breath is. You should get really familiar with it, and see how smoothly it can go.

This mind has limited life, limited body. Limited means conditioned, as each of us are. It continues as an identity for a while. That means you can say, "Yes, this is me. Today is myself. Yes, that was my self a year ago." This continuity, remembrance of continuity, even if it's one hundred years on this earth, is not just your one hundred years of life, but infinite years involved in your one hundred years. This one hundred years are the maximum length of our life, temporarily talking. It could be one hour, one moment, with infinite time involved in one hour or one moment. I say this because the awakened nature of our life every day has no need to think about the past or even the future possibilities. Staying with the present moment connects it with infinite time, as its own quality. This word, "infinite", has a kind of sweet flavor for you, but it is a very scary time. If you experience it your ego will be destroyed immediately. "Ego" means the self-made notion of self identity, which can become like vapor immediately. So it is in kind of a dangerous state. You don't know if your life is eternal, or even shorter than a moment. The length doesn't matter, but the quality of it, how you experience it, is the point.

An ordinary, common thing is not exciting, although when you take a good, close look, an ordinary thing is very precious. The fact that we keep the same identical existence in time/space is the greatest mystery. Honest and obedient, the body is a very wonderful thing to have, in terms of seeing, recognition, and keeping your identity, even though it manifests powerfully and slowly, and eventually you come to an end. Life is nothing but birth and growth, and maintaining and nourishing, and flourishing and ripening, and you come to cessation. In visible form, you come to nothing. Your elements return to various places. We say that is extinction.

To feel that some day, any time, it can happen, my own death, is really scary. But the subject we are facing is this kind of subject. You can also ask yourself, "Why do I have to exist?" It's a subject which goes beyond death. If I die now, that's it. Everything is closed. If you still have some regret, you will have to live longer. If you wish to live longer, you will, because you have something to do.

The one who goes is rather the lucky one. The ones who remain and face the death of a loved one are actually very miserable, wondering whether that person is coming back or not. We don't know. We hope they come back, but they have no chance to tell you if they're coming back or not. We hear many funny stories. In the corner of the room spirits are kind of looking at you, and saying, "Hi, we are here." We don't know if it's true or not, but people conk out for a few hours and come back to their body, sometimes leaving the body, and rushing back to their old body to continue the hardship of life again. You must have such experiences. I do.

Does God exist?

A serious young man came to Buddha's assembly, wishing to find out whether this world continues after death, or after many lives. He found that nobody talked about this in the assembly. His name was Malunkyaputta. One of the elders said, "It has been said that this kind of subject causes endless argument. It doesn't do any good in daily life, so we quit talking about it." The young man replied, "Buddha is a wise, enlightened person, so he must know the answer." Finally, he came face to face with the Buddha, saying, "If you don't answer me about this subject, I'm going away tomorrow." Buddha replied, "Did I promise to discuss this when you came to me?" "No, you didn't." So Buddha began by saying, "This question comes from a person who wants to know everything first, and then begin practice." He went on, "Everything is fine now, so you can sit in peace. You are like a person who is in the woods, and accidentally was shot by a hunter with a paralyzing arrow, and begins to ask, 'Who shot me? Was this arrow for hunting deer? What kind of material is this arrow? Is it made of wood or bamboo? The arrow head in my body, is it agate or quartz or iron? What was on it? Was there nothing on it or was there poison?' Before knowing everything, you might die. First thing, you have to pull it out, and then discuss it."

Day to day, we have so many subjects to care about and deal with immediately. Whether we can deal with our reality accurately, immediately, properly, that is the very immediate subject. After long, long argument and debate on whether God exists or not, we still have the same subject. You might say it is your own real father or mother who brought you onto this earth and breathes with you every moment. If you feel and discover what is meant by God's presence, for you, you do not bring up this kind of silly question of whether or not God exists. It is the first knowledge of people who, as children, believe and have confidence in the presence of a creator and created beings. But today, many modern people feel that the creator was actually a created existence. One morning we picked up a young hitchhiker who started to talk about this very subject. "Actually, human beings created God." And I said, "Oh? I thought it was the other way around." Some atheists have this perspective, that from mythological time, humans projected their first reason for existence, and finally brought in God as the first origin of everything's existence. So here we have a very big problem. People who never have seen or had a connection with so-called "God" cannot say, "Yes, He exists, doesn't, or might exist, or has existed, or He's resting, or sleeping upstairs," or something like that. It is very difficult to prove existence.

This question of God's existence faces toward the outside, but actually, it comes back to each of us to ask whether we, ourselves, really exist or not. It sounds as if the answer is "yes" or "no," fully one hundred per cent "yes," on one hand, and, on the other hand, one hundred per cent "no." Actually, both are able to be true. Whether you settle on "yes" or settle on "no," things are still the same.

One day a young American man came to my master's temple and had a direct encounter with him. Later, my master's wife, who had listened as she served tea, told me about it. The American asked, "Do you think God exists, or not?" My master answered, "He must exist. He certainly must exist." The man said, "Oh? I thought Buddhists didn't speak about God. That's the very thing I wanted to hear. But why did you say, 'must exist"? My master answered, "It is very convenient." He wasn't joking. He always spoke like that to me. "Only when you become very helpless, you scream for His help. Certainly He comes and says, 'See I told you. You didn't hear me. Correct your attitude!' At that moment things turn out pretty good. But when you are in good condition, you don't even think about Him." That is what he meant by "convenient."

I am sort of Japanese. I have roots in Japan, so I go back to contemplate where my root is, and I find there are many gods in Japan. And it finally settled down to the belief that they all originated from one God. As you know, Shintoism is the nation's unspoken belief. From mythological times, we have believed God existed. So I do not have any question or doubt about it, even though I haven't met Him. There are many names, but the actual one doesn't have a name. It is present in the future, and fills wherever space and time is. It is that kind of presence, I have no doubt of that. I don't know anything about it, but I have no doubt about it.

DENKO·E SESSHIN

ASSEMBLY ON THE TRANSMISSION OF LIGHT

Chapter 15

Light

"At the very beginning of practice, faith in yourself is absolutely necessary. It is the content of way-seeking mind."

Light

Very happy to join you in sesshin. Almost every autumn we have Denko-e sesshin here. We speak of "denko," transmission of light. What kind of light? It is something which shines, sometimes externally, sometimes internally. There is brightness which you sense within your body, and bright light outside of your body. You sense it's in you and in all things outside of you. It is burning and shedding light.

The light that is transmitted comes out of people. I don't see it myself, in me, but I see it in others. This light is not always constant. Like a firefly, the light is generated inside. I don't know what is the substance of it, but each one of us is a kind of potential way-seeker, and at the same time our everyday lives are precisely related to the support of innumerable others who sustain our individual lives. Our individual existence must be returning the same amount of energy to those others. I don't know what this all means, how far it reaches, but it is true that each person carries a life which exchanges energy in some kind of community. Of course, if the sun didn't exist, none of us could live, so in that sense, the sun is constantly related to you. In the same way the movement of this galaxy, stars, and planets, is keeping this earth together. It's beyond my understanding, but I suspect the whole thing is actually one fantastic dynamic, embedded in us before we knew it.

When the moon and stars stop shining, what do you depend on to live? Your eyes are useless at that moment. You might make a fire, or turn on the electricity, but even that is closely related to sunlight. In our heart, according to the Upanishads, is Atman, and in the center of Atman are a billion Atmans. And in there is a light. Atman shines, so we notice each other, and this Atman is a small version of this big universe, which is called Brahman. And this Brahman and Atman are actually identical in their essence. That is how the Upanishads talk about Atman.

Sensing the Light Within You

When you touch your body, you feel warmth. Something is burning, and connected with this thing that's burning, there is a light. Your eyes are rather like a window of this inner light. If you are discouraged, or very ill, your eyes don't show light. When you are full of hope, full of vitality, inside and outside, your eyes shine. Partly, it could be recognition of something, and being recognized by it. Faith, no doubt, has something to do with this shine of eyes. They go together. Sensing the light within you is really the same as expecting a new day tomorrow. If there is a future, there is a light coming from it.

Now, we are practicing sitting. It looks like nothing is happening, but that is just an outlook, because there is no obvious movement or visible product, yet you know lots is happening. You are recognizing, observing, your mind phenomena, playing a video of your own life story, like going into a huge warehouse where everything is in disorder. Things are thrown into it, like here are some pots, some books, and there are ghost-like people. Noticing what's in there is like taking a journey into yourself, looking into your past and re-examining, reviewing all those experiences. You open all doors and entrances of this storage room and let the sunlight in. It shines into the dark corners and puts thing in order. Sitting is like that. It makes the wind go through and the light shine in. This is not just your own short life, this life; it involves the roots, the previous lives of your ancestors.

Most of the time my sitting is utterly dark, and very warm. It feels like a fermented junkyard. Yet once in a while a forgotten jewel is in there. When I pull it out, it shines. I often feel that the action of zazen saves me from so much heaviness of life. It brings me back to where I started. After about five or six sittings, my body feels very energized.

Practice Alone

Being born, all of a sudden, without knowing that we are going to be given life on this earth, even though our parents care for us and we are given necessities and education, still, we are basically alone. Yet, growing up on this earth, we come to think that actually we are not alone. We have many friends, family, and all other beings around us, so we forget that we exist alone. At birth, and again at the time when you pass on, you realize that you've been alone from beginning to end. Sometimes it feels fine to be always alone, but most of the time we feel loneliness instead of confidence. It's like, "Nobody knows me and I do not know myself."

And yet, true religion is totally accomplished only by yourself. You don't need anybody else besides you. So if you do not have accurate, proper guidance for your spiritual seeking, you had better practice alone, even if you don't have a guiding torch to measure your position. Your way-mind itself is a torch, burning fire. Even if it only shines around you, or sometimes just inside of your body, you are joining in the long history of spiritual seeking. All world religions today speak of the importance of the life of the individual, and, at the same time, all agree the life of others is as important as your own life. That is the underlying essence of modern religion.

From the very first zazen, even if you live full of delusions and problems, from the sprouting of your great compassion, your zazen becomes zazen. Your physical body is the ground where knowledge and understanding arise. They are not given to you, but discovered from you, as you receive or reflect on teaching. Otherwise, there is no teaching coming to you. The treasure is within you. Teaching doesn't come from outside of you. Your heart beat, your breathing, are not all that are within you, some cosmic reality is there and you are experiencing it. There is no teacher, so to speak, no student. Teacher and student are just phenomena. To say, "Someone taught me" or "I taught somebody" is just a reminder of something going on.

I know that my life here, as an individual entity, is not accidental. We can understand that without our parents, and endless parents before us, our lives would not be here, but when we go into our own biological presence, and then go way, way back, it gets too complicated, so we don't try to know it. One life is like a little spring plum blossom, blooming on an aged, aged plum tree. The tree has moss all over it and you are blooming at the tip of a little green new branch. So you look around, in this stage of life, and notice we all look alike. Whether man or woman doesn't matter. There are two eyes, something sitting in the middle of the face, and each body, from a young baby to an aged person about to step into the coffin, all look quite similar. Remembering how your life has continued from the very far past up to today's life here, is too profound, too miraculous. You don't want to think about it. Thinking about the future, where you might be, where you might live, is even more impossible.

At the very beginning of practice, faith in yourself is absolutely necessary. It is the content of way-seeking mind.

Chapter 16

Listen to the Truth

"If there are any misunderstandings about what is called Zen life or Buddhist life, I'd like to clear them up and reassure you that however you are is the way you should be."

Listen to the Truth

Practice is very individual, but if you get lost in it your nature is not developing; you are sealed in with conceit, so you don't hear anything from anybody else. That's what it means to be "lost." You don't sense that there is something else existing besides you. Practice of zazen can be very dangerous in that way, when people just sit by themselves and do not communicate. This is called "kuhu" zazen, which means you are very good at encouraging your intuition to gather every necessary faculty to practice. "Kuhu" zazen is when you pound your body and mind for zazen. You see your body as very lazy and dull so you pound your energy to manifest properly.

"Sanchi manpo," which means to plunge into the teacher and listen to the truth, encourages you to avoid the danger of getting into a conceited state. Simply speaking, it's a very ordinary teaching. You renew yourself totally every moment and don't get caught sleeping in a conceptual space. "Sanchi manpo" frees you from any kind of identity trap.

In the monastery of Buddha's order the main task of monks and nuns, inside of the monastery or nunnery, was silence. When it was necessary there was very sincere discussion, Dharma discussion, but metaphysical discussion was prohibited because it was endless and could become a reason for an order to separate. An example of such a discussion would be whether or not this world, this universe, ends some day. In Buddha's time, they discussed whether this universe is utterly, endlessly open, or somewhat closed, and whether the Tathagata ends its life or not. But such discussion never satisfies, instead, we practice living, and staying awake.

Long, deep silence, which contains everything in each person, is very important, even though it contains a bundle of problems inside. To keep these many problems intact, is basically what we are, but if we continue not expressing them to others we cause more problems. At the same time, when you talk, it should be done by a loving mind, instead of a sharp knife or arrow. Words are powerful, and when the listener is ready to know what you want to communicate, it becomes very important for you to talk. It is said, "Talking should be done out of compassion, with wisdom regarding when and how to talk." It is very important, as a gift to others, even if it is an utterly critical word, it is important to present it.

The technique of one person talking, in a group, is a skilled technique. Otherwise, everybody would talk all at once, and you'd listen to everyone all at once, and you'd get nothing. When I talk, if I am very confused, you will know I am very confused. So this way, the way of one person talking, is economy of time and space, practiced for centuries. We call it "ugo-noshu." "Crow find the dead deer." The crows all cry and whoever comes first finds it. It looks like I came first, so this robe is a sign of trust, not my trust in myself, but the trust of society in the robe. I am so happy to do this, but alas, underneath the robe is an empty being. Nothing exists.

Sanchi Manpo and Dokusan

"Sanchi" means entering into the space, the room, of the teacher, like "sanZen." "Manpo" is listening to the Dharma. "San" is something going in, like a tree growing into the blue sky. It is a student coming into the dokusan room without a textbook or a friend, going all alone to enter the room where someone is waiting for you, to meet with you. That is the specific meaning of "sanchi manpo." More generally, it is understood that, whether in sitting, or doing other things, whatever you learn from the situation, that is "manpo." It is listening and seeing truth. Sanchi manpo and making a great effort to practice zazen, these two always go together.

"Dokusan," a personal, individual interview, is not a confession ceremony, or putting problems out in public. Dokusan is not like that. When you feel you must do dokusan, I am waiting. If no necessity appears, that is perfectly fine. Dokusan can call you anytime, as you are always ready for you. In our zazen practice here, to be alone some place outside, is dokusan. To sit on your seat is dokusan. A small job like cutting vegetables, is dokusan. The whole world is waiting and waiting and waiting for you, for your complete, perfect enlightenment. It's been so long, very long. And yet, one flash of the perfect enlightenment at the very beginning of right practice means that all of us are Anuttara-samyaksambodhi, "perfect, supreme enlightenment," and all of us are always in Nirvana. That is what unconditioned Nirvana is. No abiding means you are always within it. You don't go out of it since there is no outside. There is no such sentient being outside of Nirvana.

I don't have any sense of training you for something. Also, we have lots of friends, brothers, sisters, parents, who are practicers, and their choice to join or not to join sesshin makes very great sense too. So if this is not training, what is it? It's not school, of course. I'm talking about the kind of sitting we are doing here. If there are any misunderstandings about what is called Zen life or Buddhist life, I'd like to clear them up and reassure you that however you are is the way you should be. However you manage your daily life, that is how it should be. I'm saying this because there is such a long traditional way of monastic practice in which sitting was done only in a closed society like a monastery. My basic intention is to really open this sitting opportunity to everybody who is ready to do it and enjoy it, with no division between monks and nuns, young and old. For some who were trained in the monastery or communal situation with a well-set schedule and regulations, it might be quite difficult that we have almost no rules. People come in and go out and there is no scolding or carrying a stick to beat you up like an old rug or dumb person. Many people say that is not sesshin, but I believe this is the real sesshin.

Even When There are no Words, There is Teaching

The question comes, "Is it important to have a lot of interviews with a teacher, or can practice be left up to zazen?" The answer is that the two biggest elements of our practice are zazen practice and "man po," learning. If a teacher sees all practicers as imperfect, he stands up as the direct teacher, and endlessly he practices with the student to complete the practice. But in zazen there is already "man po"; in shikantaza there is complete "man po." This means there is no teaching in the perfect world, no teacher or student. With complete understanding of what is the enlightened one, Buddha can speak and all Buddhas listen without any sense of, "He's teaching me," or "We are listening to him." Speaking and listening have the same quality as many of the sounds around us. (A duck is quacking outside.) That voice you can understand, even if it is not a human word. That sound of kitchen (chopping, ringing of pans) you can understand, even if it is not formal human language. Even when there are no words, there is teaching, so it is a little awkward to take the opportunity to speak. The whole thing is a little dusty. Without human language, all trees and all grasses know each other completely, and they are saying, "Let's not think whether we know each other or not. We already do."

Without destroying silence, to speak or play music is a very hard thing. When you paint a picture, whether on canvas or rice paper, it's very hard to feel what the paper wants. It's strange to say it, but when you feel how the paper wants to be touched, that feeling is instantaneously experienced, so there is no problem in sensing what the paper wants to be done. To lower the dimension from three to one, for instance, to let the round cubic moon appear on the flat paper, is quite difficult. Even more difficult is letting people feel the moon more than by seeing the actual moon. This is not just the artist's job. It is everyone's job. We are constantly experiencing the inner joy or suffering of life and sharing it with other people. This is how we are living. We are expressing what has to be expressed, listening to what should be listened to. We are not just watching, or seeing, or hearing, but catching the real thing which is quite invisible but has to be shared. To express crystal transparent light with colors and sounds is very hard, almost impossible. Using color to express no color is a hard thing, but, when we look at our life closely, we are often doing it.

Complete manpo and complete zazen, pure listening to the Dharma and pure zazen, are not separate things. They are one thing. In visible form, everyone is teacher and everyone is student. You cannot say, "I am just a student," and I don't say, "I'm the teacher." All of us should understand a deeper sense of teacher and student. Maybe you are the teacher and I am a little student. I don't think teacher and student is shepherd and sheep, or a man putting a ring in a cow's nose. From Dhammapada, from Buddha's word, how to practice is to live what is taught. By doing so, you become so. Doing so, you realize you are so. By doing something, you know who you are, what you are. Your practice should walk along like a rhinoceros which is fleeing the field. Your practice should be like a dragon, or salmon, which leaps upstream in the water, or a bird which is freed from the cage. Even when you are free from the cage, the huge sky tells you there are different kinds of cages which you can appreciate. "Cage" is not such a good word, rather, "way to live." To learn how you are is the most direct teaching.

Kyoju

"Kyo" means teaching, or "to teach." "Kyoju" is, with no separation, directly, you hand something down to another existence. An amazing thing is that the something which is supposed to move from one to another, doesn't retain the same form. When you teach someone how to cook, giving the recipe, instruction, and practicing together, the result is never the same. The guest knows that this is not the mother's, but the daughter's, work. This is how Dharma is transmitted from generation to generation and still is not the same as before. And yet A doesn't say it is different, and B says it is the same as A. When you go to the market to pick out some squash, they look similar but when you look closely each squash is a little different.

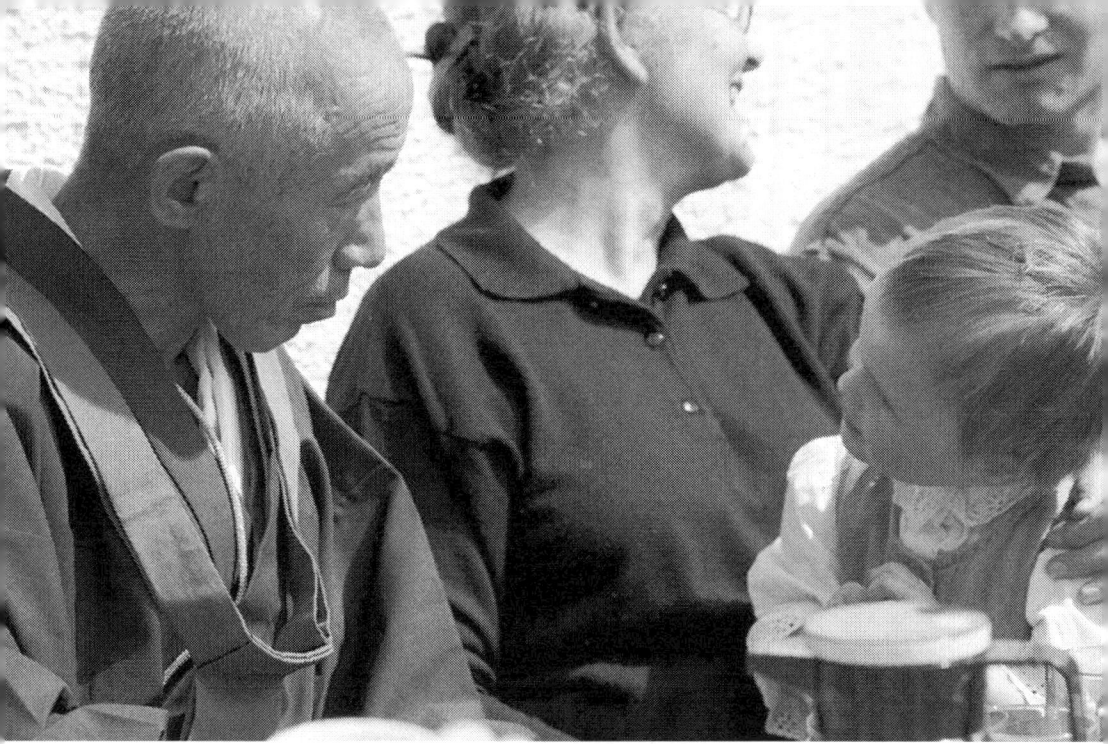

Chapter 17

Menju: Face to Face Transmission

"The person you are facing is light touching you."

Menju, Face-to-Face Transmission

What is very important about "menju" is that when you are one of two existences, and you meet and receive something, you do not just receive it, you also accept yourself. Menju is acceptance of self, through acceptance of another. The one who is giving, handing down, is not someone else. Complete trust exists, as if you are him or her, whether teacher or student, so that the giving and receiving, through another's body, is actually the same. You could say the student and teacher don't exist as teacher and student, just, something is going on.

This "men" is a very strong word. It's a face, a presence. When you see the real face, the face which is not real disappears, and the face which is real appears. If we do not see the real face, it is because we do not want to see it. A different word for "face" might be "existence." It's not reflection, or imagination. To see a real face in the mirror of nothing is using the sharpest and most merciless sword, like facing death. It's so fine, you don't feel it going through. Transmission is like this. It has to be done by yourself before it is done.

Dogen Zenji and Menju

In Shobogenzo, Dogen describes the meeting where Shakyamuni Buddha holds up the udumbara blossom and blinks his eyes. At that moment, Mahakashyapa, his face becoming completely transformed, smiles. Buddha announces, "The wondrous mind of Nirvana is given to Mahakashyapa and belongs to Mahakashyapa." Dogen picked up this original idea of transmission of the Dharma and discussed this very delicate meeting called "menju."

Dogen Zenji lived in the 13th Century in Japan. He was born in 1200 and died at Eiheiji at 54. His mother died when he was about three, his father when he was eight. He entered a temple at age 13. Two years later he came down the mountain to the city of Kyoto, and joined the Rinzai master Eisai Zenji, whose successor, MyoZen, took him to China when he was 23. For three years he traveled around China, finally coming to the gate of Tiantong Mountain. He saw a small figure inside the temple. Taking the formal entrance to the Dharma Hall, where the small figure waited, Dogen bowed on the floor 100 times, to Tiantong Rujing, who transmitted the Dharma to him, saying, "Last night Manjusuri Bodhisattva appeared to tell me this would happen. Welcome!" Dogen's way-mind had been arising since he was small and he had a fatalistic and natural feeling about this meeting. He asked, "May I come to you anytime, taking off all masks, may I come with my bare existence?" Rujing replied, "From now on, without the limitation of time, day or night, with robe or without robe, I will not hesitate to meet with you, who ask for a path. Like a grandfather and grandson, no formality." Maybe everyone has had this kind of experience, a real meeting with another person, mutual acceptance without any effort.

We have a record (Note: Kobun is translating from a tattered book, filled with his own copious notes.) of some fifty questions and answers between Dogen and Rujing. It shows that Dogen prepared many kinds of hammers and tried to hit the gong from many different directions. This record tells us that the great way to Buddha Patriarch is only in face giving, face receiving. There is nothing else, nothing more, nothing less. This face giving is to face your own face, with joy, with pleasure, with faith, to actively receive it.

It is very important to look at the background of written material. Even though it tells the truth in universal terms, still, we have to see what kind of conditions brought us this writing. We easily criticize with our mind in the present, so we should remember how new these ideas were in Dogen's time. It was a time of change in Japan, the capitol was moved from Kyoto to Kamakura. The river Kamo, which cut through the center of Kyoto, was never clear, Dogen wrote, because it was polluted with blood and dirt from fierce fighting. Most of Dogen's life he was staring at a situation of fighting and sickness. His father had been a governor but was smashed by a political movement, kind of purged. Dogen was expected to take over some responsibility for his family, but his life took a very different course.

He never appeared in the city. The people who kept Dogen's materials were the ones who went up the high mountain to see him. His life was direct and straight in a way that present man cannot feel or deal with. He had been a monk from age thirteen and, until his death day, never knew a woman. He almost never talked about women, so it is sometimes difficult for women to study this material. An example of the way he spoke about love is, "To deeply consider about gratitude, grateful love, is to throw away grateful love." He is saying, to free the object from one's attachment is to keep it.

Dogen wrote, "The basic discipline of Shobogenzo, Treasure House of True Dharma Eye, is face transmission, BuddhaBuddha, Patriarch-Patriarch." In order to understand what this "menju, face-to-face transmission," is, I'd like to speak about the contents of menju. In the word, itself, there is some feeling of form, a front side and a back side. There are two figures, and there is a meeting. In every kind of meeting you can speak of menju, but what makes this menju possible? We have talked about how if you want your knowledge to continue, there has to be somebody to maintain your knowledge. In music, painting, cooking, sewing, sweeping, mechanics, pottery, there is the idea of transmission of skill and knowledge with direct continuity from one to another in actual history, actual time advancing, combined with a wish to do it. This particular word, "menju," which is used in Zen tradition, refers to succession of spirit. There can be similar forms which cannot be called, "menju."

Dogen's Four Stages of Way-Seeking Mind

Understanding menju is helpful when discussing the arising of way-seeking mind. This analogy is not so good, but, what if an old beggar stands at your door and asks for something.

If you cannot immediately see what he wants, menju isn't accomplished. If you ask, "What can I do?" it is already too late. Maybe he is hungry or cold because he stands at your door. If he is just kidding, you say, "Go next door. You don't need anything." Way-seeking mind is thirsty mind, or unfulfilled mind, needing something, like the beggar. You cannot do anything but follow it. Before way-seeking mind appears, intellect guides your existence. Intellect tells you, "Life should be like this, the family tradition is this, we should go this way." Because man is not separated from society, these thoughts are fine, but they don't help you to find your basic nature, your basic ability which you discover and which helps you respect your life, how you want to be on this earth.

In Dogen's terms, way-seeking mind is called "arising mind, starting mind, discovered mind, or opened mind." Then there is "practice, awakening, and nirvana." These are the four stages: Arising mind, practice, awakening, nirvana. This is like four parts of a circle, maybe four faces of a house. It describes the way man's mind constructs or understands what the basic function of life is. In children's terms it can be called teaching, practice, faith, and confirmation. For Dogen Zenji arising mind, ongoing practice, constant awakening, and perfect, utmost peace, these four are visible in the development, the advance, of life.

Each one of the four stages includes the other three, so if you speak of arising mind, the other three are there, and when you speak of practice, arising mind is in it. When you speak of awakening, the result, purpose, or virtue, is in it. These stages are not static. They are always contained in each individual's existence. It is a very dynamic way to see what religious life is, in each day, each hour, each moment. This kind of life is ready to be met with, to be found, by anything or anybody, by itself, or by all. This is what menju makes possible. It is like a seed which is in the ground, and at the right time and right place the sunshine hits, raindrop hits. That is how menju works. It doesn't matter whether it is a man or woman; this readiness can happen at any time. But if it doesn't happen, it is the same as if nothing is happening. Seeds which are stored in a dark place, or stored on the highway asphalt, are not much different. Readiness is very important.

So the subject of meeting with a fitting teacher, or fitting disciple, is very important. The right student, right teacher, right situation, right conditions, are all created by way-seeking mind. Way-seeking mind is very blind, but it can feel "right way" or "wrong way." It is not intellect. You feel it. If it is not the right place, way-seeking mind withdraws; if it is right, way-seeking mind stays. Are you always crying for something? Menju is the mutual acceptance which ceases the crying of way-seeking mind, because it is done. It is done. You mutually feel so.

Both Nyojo (Japanese name of Rujing) and Dogen Zenji, in their meeting at Tendo (Tiantong) Mountain, were at a very ripened stage to meet, even though they didn't know they were coming close. Manjushri appeared in Nyojo's dream, as I have said. If your way-mind is very alert, this kind of thing is usual. You sense something before the physical meeting, not that something is coming, but your own readiness. Dogen described it, "Song of bamboo is beautiful but it doesn't appear alone. It is waiting to meet with the spring wind." When a flower blooms, it is powerful, by itself. At the same time, you feel the great power of spring. Dogen wasn't surprised that Nyojo was waiting for him, yet he was deeply inspired. He had great certainty because he was ready to drop, to flourish. His whole body and mind were filled with emotion, beginning very hard practice from that point. In a sense Dogen Zenji's way-seeking mind, from age 13 to 25, was a crazy mind, like burning fire. He couldn't control it. Master Nyojo had to take care of this burning fire.

The flame of this fire contained various historical questions, for instance, "Why were seven Buddhas transmitted the Dharma before Shakyamuni?" Nyojo answered, "The Dharma is not transmitted just one way." When the tulip blooms right now, it tells its own past history, while fully expressing that there is a future. When you translate a very old text, with unfamiliar vocabulary, you have to find that each of our lives is composed of a quite old vocabulary. For instance a California poppy which grew 200 years ago is very similar to present day poppies.

Menju and Way-Seeking Mind.

I have been thinking about whether it is possible to put this relation of face-to-face transmission into one's everyday practice. One could explain it as changing the syllables in a sentence, changing the sentence without losing the matter with which it is concerned. Transmission is not only transmission of form, but of something which connects one to another. Nowadays people have very strong way-mind. Unless it discovers itself through something or with something, it cannot be satisfied, so this strong way-seeking mind travels from one situation to another. This happened with Dogen Zenji for many years, and finally he crossed the ocean and went into another country. China gave an opportunity for Dogen to recognize his own way-seeking mind. Then Master Rujing said, "Go home. Go home. Live in the countryside." That's very kind advice. The question is, how can one maintain this transmission? It is once a lifetime. It is one meeting, one period. A period is like one life. It expresses being-in-time. If you miss the one meeting, until the next life you have to wait.

It can be said that the practice of meditation actually contains menju. It means not just "face to face," but also, "mind to mind, eye to eye, hand to hand." "Ju" is direct giving and acceptance, which is similar to your relationship with your sitting meditation. Just by reading about it, imagining it, unless you do it, you cannot understand meditation. With your body you understand, by your own experience, which, surprisingly, is not like you supposed or imagined. In fact, it is the same as your ordinary experience, but also very different. Even when people practice meditation with a great ambition to be enlightened, when enlightenment happens, they are surprised that it's nothing special. If one strives hard and reaches the final destination, one has to find that everyone is already there.

Tozan's Experience of Menju

Way-seeking mind does not need to move from one place to another. Tozan discussed this point. This young monk said to his master, Unman, "Show me your truth." The answer was, "Thus, this, so" or better English would be "This is it," or "That's it." Tozan didn't understand this. So the master said, "Why don't you do hen san? Go away and see the world a little more, then come back." "Hen san," is "universal visiting." It means that way-seeking mind is never satisfied until it covers the whole universe. So Tozan decided to do hen san because he couldn't see the "shin," the "truth" of the master. The master added, "Take it easy. If I express the truth, you will regret it and I will regret it." So Tozan went on travelling practice. Finally, a time came when he was crossing a river on a little log bridge, and the current became very calm. Stepping carefully and looking down into the bottom of the water, Tozan saw something in the bottom of the calm water. At that moment, instead of crossing the river, he turned around and came back to his master, Ungan, bowing a few times in front of him. "Thank you! If you had answered me that time, I may not have had this experience." This kind of menju exists. Like an electric switch goes on, and a few minutes later, it appears.

Yet, what happened to Tozan can never replace your own experience. You don't ask someone to live your life. Your life is your life, and another's life is another's life. You don't say, "Please come into my body and live for me." Do not misunderstand transmission. The face and eye of the self is not just the face and eye of yourself. The face and eye of the Tathagata, is "Thus is so," "Nothing but it." Tathagata is not somebody floating in the air. He is the one who is "thus come and thus gone," and the one who never comes and never goes. Tathagata has those two sides. This is Tathagata's existence. Dogen says, "What face/eye of the Buddha means, is moving this face, these eyes to Tathagata, you make Tathagata yourself." What a strange way Dogen speaks. Moving this eye and putting it into the Tathagata is one way to see the other side of the transmission, which means you are also putting Tathagata's eye into your eye. You become yourself. It is mutual. But you have to have another being.

Prostration, Gassho, and Bow

Prostration, gassho, and bow are very unfamiliar gestures for most of us. But these actions have something to do with expressing yourself toward somebody as a realization of sameness. You meet this person as yourself. Since you cannot put your hand inside your body, it appears in "gassho." In other words, there is no one out there. It's all yourself. One side is you, one side is the person who is prostrated. You do not feel alone at all. One hand alone doesn't feel anything. This hand feels this hand, this hand feels this hand, all at the same time. The person you are facing is light touching you. Prostration is completely without any hestitation or question, even if you have a bundle of doubts and questions, you throw that doubt in front. Prostration is a very profound practice, and it is as important as your sitting practice. Pay attention.

Chapter 18

Many Kinds of Transmission

"If you are the one being baptized, you don't need to understand, just be there and cleanse yourself."

Many Kinds of Transmission

Another way to approach the subject of menju is to say that it is happening all the time, during your entire life. It is a little shaky when you say, "Maybe this is it." But there is the feeling that it's happening all the time, no matter whether you are happy or unhappy, whether it's daytime or nighttime, whether you recognize it or not.

This "men," this face, can be understood as Bodhidharma's word, meaning it can be seen as mind, directly pointing to another mind. Mind to mind, at this point, is menju. There can be "shinju", "body to body," "genju," "eye to eye." To hand something to somebody is transmission, too. For example, if I didn't make this cup, but the one who made it handed it to me, I could experience it fully. But in the kind of transmission we are talking about, the one who made this cup doesn't give it to me, but transmits something else which makes it possible for me to make this. Maybe I can make another kind of cup in the same manner, and not just enjoy the after-process of this existence. If I practice a little, by one glance I may know some brief knowledge about what kind of clay, what kind of glaze, what kind of heat, was required. To really know how this cup appeared is to retrace the efforts of making it. It is not just retracing the knowledge of how to make it, imagining how it went, but step by step you learn by your hand.

Face to face means actual action. You learn painting, calligraphy, carpentry, cooking, sewing, even sweeping or taking a bath, when you do it. So in the broader sense of menju we are within it. Family life is one great opportunity of menju, how to live, how to form ourselves. This subject is understood through our sense of practice.

The Origin of Menju

The teacher and student or master and disciple relation was discussed by Dogen Zenji. Shakyamuni Buddha and Mahakashyapa, Rujing and Dogen, the Fifth Patriarch and Sixth Patriarch, are all fragrant stories concerning this subject of menju.

According to the literature, Mahakashyapa seems to be a very important existence in Buddha's time, with a big family and a group of followers. On one occasion, for the first time, Buddha had Mahakashyapa sit beside him, much to the confusion of Buddha's followers and the surprise of Mahakashyapa, since before that time, even though he taught followers how to be and how to practice, Buddha had remained alone. He would say, "No one understands fully what I am, what I teach." But after many meetings with Brahmins here and there, he felt something was happening, so on the morning when Mahakashyapa moved toward him, Buddha caught such a sense. And to Mahakashyapa, the cognition appeared, "This is my teacher, I am his follower." Yet many of his followers didn't know what he was thinking, and it looked very strange to them. For one thing, both Mahakashyapa and Shakyamuni Buddha were quite old. From a disciple of Mahakashyapa the question appeared, "What's happening there?" Catching the question, Mahakashyapa announced, "This is my teacher. From now on I am a student of this man." Menju is like this.

This occasion, which is seen as the origin of menju, and usually thought of as a dramatic happening, seems like a natural event when you look closely at how Mahakashyapa often met with Buddha and others who came around. It seems natural that he would receive transmission from Buddha. Also, we have to be aware that there is a question whether Mahakashyapa, alone, received transmission. We can think about this in terms of the conditions which provide opportunities. For instance, if dust didn't exist, there would be no opportunity for a cloud to form. Water and particles are necessary to form a cloud in the sky. In the same way, it was a fortunate occasion for Mahakashyapa to exist close to the Buddha. You can say that Mahakashyapa was like an extended body of Shakyamuni, or Shakyamuni was like an extended body of Mahakashyapa.

Ananda was like the exposed brain of Buddha. He was always present when Buddha was meeting with people, a fantastic tape recorder who, years later, could remember everything that was said, what kind of day it was, etc. After Shakyamuni Buddha passed away, Ananda asked Mahakashyapa to clarify, with the question, "What else was happening there besides transmitting a robe to you?" (As you know, the robe is a symbol of menju, completing transmission.) Mahakashyapa immediately called back to Ananda, "Let the poles fall down all together." In dharma combat, at that time, they would put up two poles, and when the discussion was done, when "A" won in Dharma combat, the flag appeared on his side, or when "B" won, a flag flew from his pole. So Mahakashyapa meant that both poles, together, should be knocked down, whereupon Ananda stood and bowed to Mahakashyapa. That was the occasion of Ananda's menju.

This menju appears in many, many ways. The Sixth Patriarch was working in the kitchen while the Fifth Patriarch stood beside him. "Is the rice polished?" asked the Fifth Patriarch and the Sixth Patriach said, "All done. Just the straining process is left." Three times the Sixth Patriarch tried to strain the rice. That night was the transmission.

In my case, there wasn't much choice, no choice. Maybe it was decided way back some time when I wasn't born yet. My feeling is that it was decided about a century ago, or something. I tried to get away from the choice, and I still try to liberate myself from the past, but I don't succeed. Nose surgery, shaving the head, growing hair, doesn't help. I didn't do nose surgery. But that kind of effort doesn't make any difference.

A new name in the morning Eko is my root master, my Dharma master, who made it possible for me to be with you. He is Hozan Koei, "Phoenix Mountain." When the transmission ceremony took place, I was still a young kid, twenty-four years old, and I was a quite naive, proud little monk! Eiheiji was a huge organization, like a military camp, and I was kind of recognized as being in a high position, so my nose grew tall, like Pinocchio.

People would say, "Great, great!" so it grew longer. A telegram came from my master in Niigata and I thought, "Oh, no, my master is sick now!" It said, "Come back! Right away!" I went to Tatsugami Roshi's room. He was a lovely master. (His nickname was, between monks, 'Toilet Slipper' which meant the big, square wooden "geta" in the toilet. His face, big and dark, looked like it.) Later I found out they had talked to each other by letter. There was to be a transmission ceremony at my home temple.

For nearly one month I was upstairs at Hojo, my master's dwelling, with a beautiful open door, wind coming through, the smell of cedar. I remember the sounds of maple leaves touching each other. I was drawing the many, many names of the Buddha ancestors, prostrating each time. You write those names on silk cloth. Then, the Great Subject of Seven Buddhas of the past, which means Shakyamuni Buddha and six before him, a galaxy of Buddhas. Shakyamuni Buddha is still a living Buddha to each of us. Facing Buddha in this galaxy is similar to facing Christ, as a medium to God. Your life is in a similar relationship to Buddha, and to the cosmic truth, so to speak. And Shisho, the third scroll, is the transmission letter, which is like an archery target, clockwise from Shakyamuni Buddha to all masters, to your own self, all connected with one line. It is like your life line goes to the past and comes back to the present, so it becomes a circle. It is like the feeling of you sitting in a circle like this, and the next person is your own master, his master is sitting there, and it goes all the way around. And when you look the other way, Shakyamuni Buddha is sitting there.

You prostrate when you write each name. I took several weeks to complete all of it. If I had a question, I would go to my master's room and present my question. "What does this mean?" "Why is this written this way?" It is very difficult material. So my suffering began from that, on the sixth of August, when I was twenty-four years old. I just did what he said and went straight back to the monastery.

Other Traditional Transmissions

There are many beautiful stories in the past. I chanced to see a TV movie about Moses, in which the fire of life comes to the rock and carves wisdom into the hard surface. Everyone knows this occasion, even though what the Commandments truly mean is not understood. The whole scene is in the light, and Moses holds the rock while the arrow of fire carves words. When Moses came back from the high mountain, holding the rock, very chaotic energy was going on. It was like an ocean of desire taking form, with wine, sex, and human bodies. In the movie, the picture of spinning energy, bringing wisdom, looked like a man and woman's bodies, their movements like the fire, the spinning fire which hit the rock.

When we see a story, so familiar, we are somewhat able to experience what those characters experienced. Jesus hung on the cross like a rabbit or frog. It was crazy, and yet it happened. We can understand through our own bodies, like when a fingertip gets hot, the whole body senses how it's feeling. When Jesus Christ cries, "Forgive them, they don't know what they are doing!" it is not someone else's story, it's our own story. In our everyday sense of our lives, it is like that. In the depths of our minds, there are always such struggles, energies meeting, sometimes very painfully, yet sometimes the pain and struggle can resolve, become very pleasant and peaceful, giving us deep happiness just to be. Great is the human mind which sealed such figures in history. Sometimes they were very bloody. The birth of something takes place always in fluid, very chaotic and painful.

Another impressive scene is baptism. It's very wild, like a primitive who is standing almost naked in fur or loin cloth, wearing it like a kesa, standing in running water. The important thing is what is happening in the people's minds. If you are the one being baptized, you don't need to understand, just be there and cleanse yourself. It's completely different from standing and watching. Imagination, even fantastic imagination, cannot reach to the actual experience. Water, wind, sunlight, they are not wet or strong, not bright or warm, but you are cold and strong and light and warm.

Someone told me about an interesting experiment with an ant and a piece of paper. They drop the ant on the paper and he goes all around, from corner to corner, cutting across the paper and crawling around over almost the whole paper. Finally he comes back to the same point where he was dropped, (he knows the path) and begins to meditate. Does he want to melt into the paper, or fly from the paper? He begins to shake his head, and starts once more over the same path. This is like a human recurance, over and over again. Now it is finished, and here it comes once again. He says, "I know this. Let's do it once again."

Chapter 19

Mind to Mind

"A new person has to go beyond tradition, find a new element, find a new form. What is now an old form was considered new, just a moment ago."

Menju is Internal

This menju, in the form of teaching, if it is discussed in a big lecture hall, people misunderstand. An example is that big Christian meeting on TV, where Billy Graham appears and gives a big, powerful speech. It's like a dance, like Hitler, or something. As you know, religion is very individual, and very particular. If all members are ready to meet on a particular subject, then a larger meeting is okay, but if people who do not know what's happening join in such a special meeting what they get is very horizontal energy. It's like party energy. You don't know what's going on, but you are having fun! Internal teaching, on the other hand, expresses a sense of particularity, it's not general or abstract, so, in order to avoid misunderstanding, we take an internal room. Zazen is a good example. You don't show your zazen to people, you just do it, whether others see it or not. You have no sense of showing it to people. Another example is your driver's license. If you collect many driver's licenses and put them in your purse, when the officer asks, "Which one is yours?" it's a job to find it. The other licenses have nothing to do with your driving. They are like other people's zazen.

This internal room teaching has some sense of secrecy, so sometimes it is called secret teaching. It's individual teaching, so there is no need to express it in public, and even if it were exposed, others would be completely blind to it. In Japan there is secrecy in dharma teaching. Did you know that? One example is their way of mixing glaze. At midnight the teacher goes into the workshop so no one, not even very advanced disciples, can see. Only the final product is exposed to people. An advanced disciple will study the method and the spirit of the process, so he begins to know what questions he wants to ask. He cuts the future with a question, opens up the future with his own learning process, so the teacher starts to feel how to guide this interest. Then, when the student is ready to put a final glaze on, the teacher begins to share what kind of glaze fits another kind of glaze. He says, "Come at midnight. You can watch me." Later the teacher watches the student.

Menju is the result of unseen communication of abilities. The abilities come first, then menju. Naturally there are struggles, since there are no two in this world the same, but menju focuses on sameness. The question is whether you can accept another's method, which is formed from the other's ability. If you are not familiar with the form of the other's ability, you may feel sick, pained, feel it is impossible to accept this. In the case of religious rituals, you may feel unfamiliar with some parts, that you cannot stand them. With others you feel good. There are many traditional forms which have become rigid, maintaining a form which was based on an ability which happened a long time ago, but it has lost it's vividness. With some forms you feel, "This is just a seashell. It's not a living thing." Living form stays with the advance of history, advance of the present moment. When you pick up a shellfish from the sea, it loses its form. To see the real form of the shellfish is to see it in its place. It's very beautiful. Once you pick it up, it loses its living form.

Menju is two lights appearing in utter darkness, or two blind people appearing in utter brightness, yet each recognizing there is another besides himself. If two lights meet in utter darkness, because there are two of them, they recognize they are light. If one light is alone in the darkness, the light doesn't recognize himself. This raises the question of a problem which sometimes happens between teachers and students, the so-called "guru's favor." Guru's favor is just an illusion. It happens when a student senses a lack of something in himself, and the guru stands like a king, with an empire of power. That isn't the right way. Ignorance didn't exist only in ancient times; ignorance also exists in the present, creating a similar condition as in former times. How to lighten this condition of ignorance is all up to you, not to the teacher. "Guru favor" is to lose yourself in the teacher. This isn't the way. You don't lose yourself. You shine a light into ancient darkness, through your teacher, other teachers, your friends, even the next generation. Once there was a young girl of great ability and empathy who had a fine old teacher, but she became mixed up with him. Whatever he spoke, she spoke. She became an old man, acting at home like an old master and finally she had to find herself in a mental hospital. A student may have empathy, ability to learn, but shouldn't change form completely. One should keep one's form. Otherwise, when one person dies, the other will have to follow. It is like a Pharaoh's death, when many had to follow.

We have talked about how meditation is a very personal, universal action, or maybe a universal, personal action, so that each of us has to have strong confidence in our own meditation. The substance is not in someone else, or somewhere else, it's here. When I talk about dangerous phenomena in religious practice, I am continuously suggesting to you that you are your own master. Otherwise a meeting will never happen; even if you live on this earth ninety or one hundred years, you will just live alone. Maybe your senses will be working but you won't feel anything. It is not a bad situation, and maybe it's a perfect situation, to be totally ignorant about what's happening. I am suggesting it is important to meet with a sensitivity to others, an ability to feel others.

What can one do to sense others? Immediate action to achieve this is impossible. You could think about it one hundred days and the solution will not come. This question also relates to what it is to do zazen. The quality and quantity is so fine, you don't recognize it is done. If there is a little crunchy element in your zazen, then you can understand, "I got it!" Sometimes when very fine music is playing, you don't feel it is music, but if it is a little difficult to listen to, you feel, "This is music." And yet there is real music which goes through you without a struggle, and you feel, "That's nothing." Many times we experience these feelings which are a little difficult to feel.

The study of menju can open broadly to this kind of concern. Menju, real meeting, goes beyond forms, so all religious concepts, symbols, doctrines fall apart when such a meeting is done. Retracing a religious form, you can never reach it, it is simply past. You are in the present and you don't return the fallen leaf to the branch. When man and man meet, or maybe man and absolute existence meet, doctrines and forms are too embarrassed to pop up between. This doesn't mean forms are useless, of course. Structures, phenomenal structures, help you remember unseen experience, so by seeing a form which is beyond you, you understand, "Oh, I used to be like that." But it is not the same as "I am like that."

We came together like this by saying it was a sesshin, twenty people were to meet. Actually, something which we don't know, happened. As soon as you say, "I know what happened," you've got some kind of form. And yet there is very subtle knowledge, certain knowledge, of what happened. If you don't remember who came, you are not so clear. Maybe your mind was off to some realm. What happens is recognized in real meeting. And in real meeting there are one hundred forms possible to be done, in different ways. So whatever form is chosen is always very refined. This is what happened here. It means nobody but you, each of you, came to this place. If you went to Sunday service in a church, maybe one hundred humankind would be existing there. Beautiful light might be coming from the stained glass window, allowing you to see people are there. What exists at that time is not those people, but just one light. If one of them recognizes it, the whole thing makes sense. If none of them recognize it, the whole thing is just complete darkness.

Menju and Two Moons

A new person has to go beyond tradition, find a new element, find a new form. What is now an old form was considered new, just a moment ago, so the emphasis of menju is the student, not the teacher. As Suzuki Roshi said, "I'm old and weak. The young should walk in front of me." Students' study practice should be vivid, looking back at tradition to see it's still there, not striving to reach to the teacher. You turn your head to see, "Oh, he's still there." In that way you practice. Words are necessary to communicate, but when you get stuck on the teaching, you lose the figures who taught it, or who is learning. You begin to lose the sense of menju. I am not saying teaching is not valuable. Many sutras are very beautiful and nice to study. What we also need to learn is beyond that, or maybe behind that. It is the one unexplainable mind, or experience, which makes the human symbols connect with us. What is calling to us is not man, it is existence, man or coyote, or waterfall.

Menju, even when there is great light, is meeting another in utter darkness, utter aloneness. Even if you see the complete perfection of all beings, it is still the same as utter darkness. So to see other beings is to say to yourself, "I am awakened. I am awakened because I see them in the dark." And the other confirms your mutual experience. When you say, "I see this," the other says to you, "I see this."

Transmission, face to face, body to body, mind to mind, is often called two moons, because an impossible thing has become possible. From one moment to another, from today to tomorrow, two moons can be seen. The meeting of two figures, a new moon and a full moon, is a unity. I became a new moon when I met with my master. My master became a new moon when he met with my grandmaster. You can think of the relation of grandfather, father and grandson. The grandson sees his father, the grandfather's son, in his grandfather. This is one way the grandson becomes the full moon and grandfather becomes a new moon. Suzuki Roshi fully expressed this when he said, "I walk slowly. You go ahead." We went walking in the rain and he said, "I am weak and old. You are young and strong. Walk in front of me. I'll follow you." This is the expression of two moons. The former moon accepts the second moon to be first and the second moon sees the first moon with the back of his head instead of with his eye.

This is the very recognition of the human mind, what changes and what doesn't change in the succession of human life. Menju is about the very essential nature of human life. When the bright full moon and new moon are together, it is a grey moon. Half of your body is bright moon, half is new moon. Confronting the future, is bright moon, facing the past is new moon. In the past is the bright full moon of Buddha Patriarchs. In the future is a new generation. You are utterly dark. If the master says, "You are utter darkness," menju is done.

Seeing the Existence Next to You

Usually it is said that religion doesn't need to discuss this kind of thing. If unity of relative and absolute is realized, that's enough. You don't need to worry about how the next person is working on it. Your whole concern is whether you are able to be in the unity of the absolute. Instead, the idea of two moons, menju, is not a relation of one to something which it is impossible to be. If you are a man on this earth, the whole thing is there. The absolute is there, before, during, and after. The subject of transmission is whether you are able to see such a man, such an existence, next to you.

Menju is completely different from practice and attainment. Practice and attainment are concerns of the human mind. Menju is concerned with the maintenance of being, the continuity of being. Our true self, our true mind, is always open to see another being, and when such a being comes to face you, you completely open and accept. At this point all sorts of ego-centered, self-centered thoughts in your mind protect true mind. Sea creatures have shells, birds have wings, what is carried by both is the same life. We suffer the clash of ego-centered ideas between people, and we enjoy it too, but our central concern is to find another existence to meet without any hindrance. This is the will of ego-centered samadhi, between you and others. Wiping away hindrances, you meet with such existences. Finally, you discover that the one you really wanted to see, to meet with, was yourself.

Why am I here?

Full enlightenment is the same as utter darkness, blind mind, blind eye, which cannot see things because they are too bright. That kind of utter darkness exists. Recognition of one's ignorance is experiencing menju with wisdom, so you meet with yourself. You have to wipe your awakening constantly, to look into your own zazen. All kinds of subjects are there. Look into your zazen with binoculars.

A difficulty is that if Dharma exists, it doesn't need man. Before earth is formed, during the formation of earth, after this earth is, maybe, broken or destroyed, Dharma is Dharma. In this sense Dharma is independent from people's existence, and yet to speak this way has no meaning, because such Dharma is in the realm of metaphysics. The important thing is that such Dharma is experienced by existence. The subject of menju relates with this Truth which goes through existence. Truth in phenomena is what we are concerned with.

This subject relates to the basic question, "Why am I here and why are all of you existing in this way?" This basic question which arises from our body and mind is the same question as why Truth exists, in other words, why Buddha appeared on this earth. What was the reason Buddha appeared on this earth? The same question can be asked: Why was there Moses, and many other prophets, as well as gods, goddesses, which have been experienced by many people? It is the question of incarnation, why he or it reincarnated into a human body. "Why am I here?" is the same question, whether it appears from a human body, or from some form in the universe which we haven't yet known. This question doesn't have any answer. Or, the answer comes before the question. Actually, in the root of the question is the answer. The answer which is acted by you is the real answer to this question. Fortunately, this question has an impersonal nature. It always includes others, so naturally, the next person comes along with you. This is why we can see people around us, truly see, not just stand beside them. We can truly understand and feel that others are the same as ourselves.

The meeting of Rujing and Dogen was like that. When you imagine Rujing, he is waiting, waiting for young Dogen in the meeting place. It was early morning and he saw young Dogen coming, burning incense in front of him. They saw each other, and Dogen began to bow, full bowing, flat on the floor. Rujing, seeing this, spoke, "Dharma gate of menju, face-to-face transmission is accomplished." Old master Rujing was famous. His nickname was Kaminari Oyaji, Thunder Dad! He had a very short temper and very quick response. If you were sleepy, he was like thunder hitting the gong. He used to hit people with his sandal if he didn't have a stick. But when Dogen arrived, Rujing's attendant was surprised because his master looked so unusually relaxed and full of tenderness. What we have to see is that transmission was already done when Dogen bowed. Seeing each other happened faster than the following body reaction. We are actually living in such a world. The thunder master is too late, light comes before him.

The udumbara flower is said to bloom once in 500 years. For the one who sees it, it is an eternal flower. In this sense, the existence of what is called "Buddhism" is in the blossom of this udumbara flower. It is always newly born. Our study of menju is whether we can see this udumbara flower. If you point to something, some phenomenon, saying, "Thus come, thus gone," that is Tathagata. "Never come, never gone," is another way to express Tathagata. In the same way, the udumbara flower never blooms, thus blooms. Dogen said, of menju, that when someone knocks on the door, the hostess is already holding the knob. When the hen is sitting on the egg, she knows when the time comes, so when the chick is knocking on the shell from inside, wiggling around, the mother knocks from the outside. From both sides they hit the shell. Menju appears in that way. The strength is balanced from both sides.

It is a delicate thing to symbolize in human words. Once we have such an experience, it is possible to understand menju. It appears in human deeds. The actions of zazen and gassho are two examples. Gassho, joining hands and bowing, is the other side of zazen. They are each a complete acceptance, not only of yourself, but of the whole thing. If acceptance is not done, you never do zazen or bowing. The bowing doesn't feel done, the zazen feels wrong. Or, zazen was done, but not done by you. Everything actually feels wrong because acceptance is not done.

Chapter 20

Facing the World

"Still, in a chaotic, confused world, splendid wisdom exists, if you are able to see it"

Facing the World

Shakyamuni Buddha described his enlightenment, saying, "Myself and great earth... sentient beings... same time accomplished the way."

Why do you keep sitting when so many poor people, sick people, need your help? Awareness and acceptance of how others are, enables you to meditate. Even if you have a stomach ache, you can meditate. Do you say, "I have a stomach ache, so I'd better not sit now" or "Is their boy crying? I must help him, even if it is time for zazen." It's a very tricky subject. A paradox. Do you take one way or the other way? Maybe this is family time, and the same time is sitting time in the Zendo. What is important is that you do what you really want to do. Standing up and doing things is straying around, sitting in full lotus is straying around, everything is straying around. But in your act of doing, you express your existence, which is not straying around.

So menju is actually everywhere, it can be holding something, meeting with people.... It was a natural thing for the Buddha when he held the spring flower, and for Mahakyashapa, who lived with him for so many years. When Buddha meditated, Mahakyashapa meditated, when Buddha got sick, Mahakyashapa became sick. Menju was mutual. This can be called current flowing, not just one way. It can be seen as alternating current. The one who appears in this flow can be called a salmon, going upstream, hitting the water once and then another time. Have you seen that? The salmon jumping is beautiful. Shakyamuni Buddha's life, before ripening, was like that. The current was against him, but for him it was not against him. He kept coming back against the flow. To follow the flow would have been against the flow. To leave from people was never leaving from people.

Now, I am in the same situation as when I was a baby. In the womb, I was in a complete world, mingled mother-father energy held me. Then one day, after I was outside the womb for a while, I saw a clear figure. This was my mother, so this other was my father. Now, I cannot discriminate who is my mother and who is my father. In woman I see father, and in young boy I see my mother. It's a crazy world. This is just a little example. Still, in a chaotic, confused world, splendid wisdom exists, if you are able to see it. On top of Everest flies exist. Cold, jewel-like rain hits the drunkard's head, too, in cold winter. This is the whole body of you.

It is good to be born as one of the moving creatures. If we were just like a rock or tree, although we achieved the same thing as Buddha did in the past, we could not share it with other beings. As creatures, we can walk, we can do innumerable things, go places, experiment with a lot of things. Instead of just flowing with change, we change things. We talk about history and the future. Sometimes we feel the future is bright, sometimes we feel helpless, with no future. Analyzing with our intellect, we conclude, looking into a newborn baby's face, "Why did I make this mistake? If the world is hopeless, why did I bring a child into it?" It feels like planting a seed on the asphalt, waiting for the car to come and run over it. Our instinct tells us there is a future, although it always falls into the course of arising, sustaining for a while, and then ceasing. The course of personal life is like that. The collective, cultural manifestation of human beings is also like that. They cycle and decay.

When I was a student at Kyoto University there was a political group called Zengakuren, a radical political group. It is a tradition for young students in Kyoto to always speak up when the government makes some ridiculous decision. The word, "Zen" suggested that it was not a long-term group, but the students couldn't stay quiet, so they set aside their major study in order to talk about national and world problems. There was a similar occurrence at the beginning of the Zen movement in Bodhidharma's time. Although Buddha's teaching began back in India, we didn't hear of Zen until Bodhidharma. It seems to me a new definition of "Zen" is needed, a new concept. Historically, this word, "Zen" was the flag of a quiet revolution. Ordinary people still feel somewhat strange about it. Zen people are called, "...a little strange, but in everyday life they are harmless to children and family." We meet with this revolution because it has something to do with the new age, the coming future.

At the same time, we have a sort of helplessness within us as to how to affect world phenomena in either a broad, or a personal, way. Criticism directed toward the world does not mean much any more. The situation is seriously advanced, so that this helplessness is not only your personal sense of danger, but that of the world, itself. What is needed is an inner revolution of oneself and the society. Society seems to be going toward health, but the direction of energy is such that we might end up in a big pit all together. For example, nationalism, today, is not a dependable consciousness. Although we are citiZens of each nation, with various racial, cultural mixtures, where governing for the maintenance of harmony within the nation is fundamental, we must still be concerned about international peace and harmony, and not destroy each other. Every being has an essential right to exist. Nobody has the right to destroy others for any reason. This right to live is a strong belief, embedded in us. You see so many problems that when your mind is not just concerned with your own personal life, you have this urge to sit with the advancing world.

A clear eye to every day has to be prepared. Each person has to have a revolution, and not depend only on tradition and custom from the past. In that sense, maybe I am one of the Zen Buddhists. But in terms of my upbringing, I have to say I didn't want to be a Zen person. I only look like one. We call it square bamboo. There are very excellent bamboo growers, as the bamboo grows they do some trick, some kind of bonsai work, putting a cast on growing, growing wild bamboo. It could be made square, triangular, go this way or that way. My upbringing made me grow a way I didn't want to. It felt comfortable, but often it became a restraint. I felt I had no life to do something. Being born into an old Zen temple with monks and nuns, two brothers, three sisters, all growing together, the tiny ones using oryoki from three years old. First come the betters. And look who goes last. It is Zen, a kind of plain belief in the new beginning. Maybe that is the particle of tradition I have received. When time goes on and things grow, one becomes two, then four, and then they stop growing, finally going into the process of cessation, preparing for renewal. This process goes on in a culture, in the largest cycle of about five hundred years. Then cultural renewal comes. When we look at the chart of Zen, or look at ourselves, we can see a so-called "environmental" cycle.

The present moment in the cycle is about coming down, down to the bottom. It is a very serious situation. A sincere answer is required. Yet, I would say it is an arising time, because the bottom is not just worse human problems, but most people are aware that we have to take care of the earth we are born with. We just have one, and everybody has to be aware of that first, before the amount of monthly income, or something. It is not somebody else's story. A new future begins in the present and it has to start, obviously, deep inside of you. Maybe it could be like the biological technique of crossing seeds to create a new kind of seed. They look like the old ones, but are different, and their quality is also different. That could be our life work.

I have lived with you for some time, but I have never talked about Zen. This is the first time. When you speak of starting an American version of Zen, I see hundreds of problems. If something new is found, it always wants to be fresh, not adapted. No name is necessary. When someone calls your given name, even your favorite name, don't you feel bad? We don't talk about this, but if someone thinks you are a certain person, don't you feel bad? I feel bad for some reason. There is a problem of wanting to be always new, and hopefully, utterly new, and utterly unrecognizable. I don't know if this is only me, or if some of you feel this way. It is a little bit scary. With constant change, you are alien to everything. But to tell the truth, we are always in such a state, and when someone calls you back to the so-called human world, you feel, "Again? Again, do I have to do this?" Still, maybe it's okay to pull you back to the human.

I wonder what we actually are. Perhaps we are very proud and vigorous, open to do whatever comes up to be done. We have been living in a very speedy time and have a lot of things to finish.

We finish some of those things each day, and have to keep ourselves going to complete all these things. When we sit like this, facing the wall for hour after hour, being supported by the presence of others, the incredible contents of sitting go with us. There is the fast coming and going of sensations, memories, which you have experienced fully, not noticing what a complicated situation you are living through. A very good friend always suggests to me, when I am going through a very difficult time, "Take it easy. Slow down and take it easy." I never could believe that taking it easy made things go easier. Now I want to say, "Take it easy" to all of you. But if I say so now, you'll get up and hit me. We are going through a very important time.

Chapter 21
Bodhisattva's Vow

"Beings are numberless; I vow to save them. Delusions are inexhaustible; I vow to end them. Dharma gates are boundless; I vow to enter them. Buddha's Way is unsurpassable; I vow to become it"

Bodhisattva's Vow

When we think of saving all beings, when one or many appear to be suffering, you cannot turn your head, your mind, away from it. That's the basis of the feeling of saving. You want to help if you can. Like with illness, whether you have the skill to deal with it, or you are an experienced surgeon, still you are not sure you can save the person. The problem in this vow is taking it literally and getting confused. Actually you can do only so much, yet you wish you could do much more. It is a gap between reality and an idea, but you do not suffer from it. The important thing is the connectedness of your mind to something, which keeps your life going with a certain tension, joy, purpose, and a sense of your worthiness to exist, so to speak. Instead of shutting your mind off from all the problems we have today, and pretending that you don't know the world, you have to deal with what you have got. If you say that you can only take care of what's inside of your skin, and what's outside of your skin is somebody else's problem, that doesn't work. Your external body, limitlessly opened, is the larger part of your body, actually. The inside of your skin is a very small part. It's a landmark, where your mind is resting. Whatever exists externally is all included in your being. It doesn't matter if it appears to be pleasant or unpleasant. The question is how to see each being in its essential nature, not how it appears and not how it should change. This may be just your temporary perception, so you have to be very clear about what exists, not how it should be.

If a need is truly urgent, death may be close. Grab the person and place them in a safe place, or if someone is sick, but has hope of recovery, you can allow that space. If the danger is not quite real, as when someone stumbles in shallow water, you have to see the reality, and give encouragement that one can walk out by themselves. When our children go away from our care, we have confidence that we and they are doing fine. You cannot help, you just watch. It's too bad that we have this ambition of perfect happiness. Unless everything is fine, our mind doesn't rest. The very best thing is to go cautiously and confidently. "Man po" is often advice from other people who experienced things before. Listen to it and just keep listening. When some kind of danger comes, you notice, "Yes, this is what they were talking about."

The enlightenment business is like becoming rich, not becoming poor. You get so much stuff, you have to take care of others. In such a state there is no sense of saving others. The problem is when "saving others" occurs without the enlightenment experience. With the judgment of good and bad, in everyday life, you may feel a little strange when you do something for somebody. Before everybody notices, you may get the sense, "I'm doing something wrong." If everybody says, "Good!" but you feel it is only somewhat good, the signal within you is where you will fiind the sense of "saving." Without judgment, you may feel okay about what you are thinking or doing even when it is not thought of as a good thing. Without doing anything, you can also save things. By your own change, things change.

It is very important not to judge. Judgment means to name and measure and finally say, "good" or "bad," or "exist," or "not exist." You still have concern for others, but free them from your judgment, and don't give them power to judge you, which saves you from judging others. In a complete mind the sense of judgment exists, but it doesn't determine the intimate relationship of two beings, which is based on compassion, and empathy. Patience is also kept by compassion, which allows time to grow and change.

When your mind cannot leave the object, it is compassion. By this compassion you are connected to other beings, not just connected, but you become one, so to speak. You become one, but you are different. The inner structure of what the relationship is, is important. Others' suffering becomes your suffering. Others' joy becomes your joy. Your life becomes very rich that way.

So the Bodhisattva's vow, the first vow, is this: "Limitless beings exist. Bodhisattvas wish to save all of them." If we just read the words, or hear the words, we need to ask ourselves, "What is this vow?" Bodhi means "awakened." Sattva, is an existing being.

So the vow a bodhisattva takes is by a somewhat awakened mind among all beings. Something is going on which is not necessarily just seeing the reality, but understanding that there are awakened beings and unawakened beings. The bodhisattva is like a seed on the asphalt. It never grows. It never accomplishes its own life. Endlessly this vow keeps bodhisattvas at work. But still a bodhisattva is a bodhisattva.

Nehan-e Sesshin

Assembly on the Parinirvana of Buddha

Chapter 22

Buddha's Enlightenment and Humankind

"When we are in the muddy road, to hate being in the muddy road doesn't do anything. The first thing is to step out of it, or find out how to walk in the muddy road. Hatred is extra. If there is some problem, kindly deal with it, take care of it yourself, in the right way."

Buddha's Enlightenment and Humankind

We have talked about Buddha's last words, when he was passing away: "It is occurring every second, to everybody, every being, as long as they exist. It is occurring every place, everywhere." Why did he say that?

Humans began to count their age of history from the recognition that others' existence is important, as well as our own existence, and this is reflected in the historical existences we call Shakyamuni Buddha, or Moses, or Christ, or Patanjali, or Lao Tsu. Many prophets were sending a signal to the whole fluid energy of humankind, "It is time to awake. You fight and kill each other because of a piece of wheat. That's not the way. There is a way to produce something to share, by cutting it into two pieces or five pieces." Before that time, the firey or flood-like energy of humankind caused constant fighting and struggling between clans and races. Although battles, or wars, have their own way of adjusting problems, by destruction, followed by harmony and the creation of a new space, there is blindness in this way. In the Vinayapitaka, the "Basket of Law," you can feel the origin of the awareness of law, in the social sense, as well as in the personal, individual sense.

As they began to recognize the importance of law, humankind rediscovered the way of meditation. In all kinds of religious texts you see clear expressions of this primitive ability, polished in particular ways. The occasion of Buddha's perfect enlightenment represents a historical consciousness reflected in one person. In the very beginning, he uttered the words saying that all living things of the great earth, at the same time, in the same way, accomplished the bodhi, the awakening. Unusual as this may sound, if you keep open your eyes from the deepest night, between two and three o'clock, just before sunlight you sense a kind of shaking of the earth, trembling of air, and you see how fantastic this is. The sun touches you and warms you up. In the same way your physical darkness, your emotional coolness, is warmed by the rising of the sun, the increasing heat of the sun, revealing shapes and colors of everything. Buddha's awakening is a very important event which makes this experience meaningful for each of us. Through the Precepts, the transmission of the Precepts, we understand what awakening is, what are the contents of awakening. It is not a past occasion. It is an occasion of the present time because way, way back, way, way beyond the past, Buddha said that his awakening reached to all, even to a time in the future. This means that his awakening has already reached to the Twentieth Century, before you were born. Maybe his awakening is still creating tomorrow's possibilities.

Looking at the morning star, Venus, opened up all of Buddha's possibilities. In the same way, that star tells us that such opening is possible in the future, too. You are watching ancient, unreal light, which is reaching to your little pull of mind. You are not watching a star, you are watching yourself. And as you watch a star, centuries of humankind are looking back at you, as you look into Buddha's eye. Take out your eye and put Buddha's eye into your socket and see what things look like. It becomes obvious that Buddha's awakening was the basis for the Precepts.

It is said that six bad monks and six bad nuns did wrong things and then came to Buddha to be told, "That is the wrong thing to do." If you were a member of the primitive order of Buddha and did one of these things, you were liberated from the sangha. Some examples of all kinds of these "wrong things" are sexual activity, masturbation, stealing, drinking, and so forth. So we have to be careful to ask if a Precept is real, beyond that kind of limited description. Is it more invisible and powerful, rejecting symbolization? Actually it's not difficult to really experience the power of the Precepts. On each occasion, your center, maybe it's from the top of your head to the bottom of your hip hole, somewhere on that line there is a compass which lets you sense, "This is the right way," or "I went a little bit off, but it's okay," or "I am lost," or "I am confused," or "I am freaked out." Negative forces with names like "sin, guilt, ignorance," are in our lives but you do not need to hate them. Keep a very empty mind. When we are in the muddy road, to hate being in the muddy road doesn't do anything. The first thing is to step out of it, or find out how to walk in the muddy road. Hatred is extra. If there is some problem, kindly deal with it, take care of it yourself, in the right way.

Usually, without recognizing the Precepts, we are living the Precepts, especially when we continue to practice meditation for a couple of months or many years. Precepts reveal themselves in the form of your practice, internally and externally. They are a discovery of one's true nature, and discovery of every being's nature. The exact way to say this is "kensho," realization of Buddha nature, but not in the limited sense of kensho. Nowadays kensho is understood as a very individual breakthrough or passing through some barrier, maybe you fall apart and discover another nature, which has been your true nature. This is a very limited understanding. With this understanding, in sesshin, or in zazen, in the Rinzai master's space, the disciple, or student, or participant, is examined as to whether this individual is aware of their true nature. But the basic significance of kensho is broader and more historical. As Dogen Zenji mentioned, the ideal time to receive the precepts is before you start to meditate in zazen. But, Dogen said, it is also fine to receive the Precepts after you have started meditation practice.

In primitive Buddhist orders, Precepts, meditation, and wisdom or sutra, together, are called "sangaku," three learnings, and one always contains the other two. So if you point to the Precepts, there is meditation and sutra wisdom in them. Without the other two, sutra, or true words, never appear. Without the other two, meditation cannot be right meditation. The emphasis on meditation is very, very strong. Especially because of this time in history, almost everyone intuitively knows it is time to meditate.

Jukai, Receiving the Precepts

"Ju" is transmission, "kai" is reminder of transmission. Buddha said to a practicing Bodhisattva, "Ten lives from now, you will achieve perfect enlightenment!" With menju, unless it happens there is no discussion about it. With jukai, it is not yet achieved; but for Buddha, it is achieved, so he can say, "You're on the track."

Some of you have received Buddha's Precepts, Bodhisattva's Precepts, as a mutual recognition of what realization of Buddhahood could be. In the original order of Buddhism, under the guidance of Shakyamuni Buddha, if one requested to join the Buddha's sangha, and renounced their family, the answer was, "Yes, you can join." That was all. Buddha's order didn't have a material position in society, except that it provided medical care and daily food. Clothing was absolutely simple. You used thrown-away, useless cloth, to wrap your body. They must have been seen as a drop-out party, or something. Certainly this was a revolutionary drop-out party. The Shakya clan was conquered by the Kosala kingdom, and they lost their land, so Gautama Buddha, one of the important rulers of the Shakya clan, renounced the world and became a drop-out.

Chapter 23

Sange

"So this word, "repentance" is personal, and it is also universal."

Sange

"Sange" is the way of repentance. You may call it confession, which may give you some idea of what it is, but I'd like you to forget what you are thinking. The Precepts are not just a personal concern, and neither is repentance. Recognition and acknowledgement of one's own personal, individual faults, mistakes, or dissatisfactions, if this occurs in reality, is a universal occasion because it is revealed in the universal scene. This reverse recognition appears in each individual's life. So this word, "repentance" is personal, and it is also universal.

When you are driving a car on the freeway, if you pass another car you feel good. When someone passes your car, you may feel something else. If you don't notice and don't feel it was one way or the other, you are enjoying driving. But once it occurs to your mind to go very fast, racing mind brings you several different emotions and sensations. In our daily life success occurs, irrespective of others' unsuccess, yet you may feel good because others are not successful. If someone else is very successful, in any way, you may come to feel left out, as if you have failed. The mistaken view is that human nature is accustomed to being negative, enjoying wrongdoing. To see the suffering of others and enjoy it is a strange thing, but we often unconsciously feel that way. At the same time, there exists a different nature in our mind. Without a sense of racing, we have a complete ability to enjoy, to congratulate others in their success, as if we did it ourselves. Enjoying the suffering of others, if it is your entire body and mind, you have no peace. Maybe only while you are sleeping do you have peace. When you are not in the race, you participate directly in whatever happens, enjoying it, or if they are painful situations, you suffer. The content of a mind which is in a state of repentance is very important. At this moment one is turning the direction of one's life. Noticing small wrong deeds of oneself can be repentance, but noticing the great suffering of all living beings is the same. What caused this suffering is realized in that mind.

Greed for fulfillment of desire, as we know, causes suffering. Once you get angry at a situation and direct your anger at someone, the situation is very hard to resolve. It is not so easy to turn your mind in another direction. These instincts of our body and mind, which are deeper than our common sense, or knowledge of how to live with people, are deep. They have deep roots. The desire to survive in your life can cause good, but this desire requires your effort to understand what kind of hindrance goes with it. Here in the end of the twentieth century this enormous energy of desire, this life strength, this desire to survive, causes fear. No one can say another war won't happen, since if an enemy appears, it is natural to fight back.

In the past, people didn't believe nations could unite. People were like insects, with insect-like consciousness. Then, about thirteen centuries ago, nations began to recognize the basic nature of all living things, through the transmission of wisdom from ancient ancestors to new generations. Now it has become more and more clear that all beings have the same life as other existences.

In human language Buddha revealed the Precepts, which are the revealed nature of the Buddha, our own true nature. This revelation brings forth the act of repentance. Your eyes start to change what you are watching; your mind is sensing something different. The eye which sees the word of wisdom is called the "Wisdom Eye," and the eye which sees the Truth within and without, is called the "Dharma Eye." The eye which sees every existence's awakening nature, that is "Buddha's Eye." We can see with many kinds of eyes. Seeing, hearing, sensing, intuiting the nature of utter truth are the functioning of our eyes, ears, and sense of touch. So we repent.

Ga shaku sho zo sho aku go

Is-sai ga kon kai san-ge.

kai yu mu shi ton jin chi.

Ju shin ku i shi sho sho

From ancient times, it goes like this: "Ga shaku sho zo sho aku go." "Aku" is wrong and evil, "go" is actions, deeds, so it says, "All wrong actions of mine from ancient time." "Ton jin chi." "Ton" is endless thirst, greed, craving. "Jin" is anger, another side of fear; anger is the sensation of separation. "Chi" is illusory knowledge which makes you feel sick, and if you give this sickness to others, you feel lonely. "Out of my beginningless greed, anger, delusion, and illusory knowledge."

"Ju shin ku i shi sho sho." "Shin" is body and its action, including mouth and speech. "Ku i " is mind, determination, will, consciousness, unconsciousness, mind-function. We may call it spirit. This "shin ku i," expressed through bodily action and speech, appears in the form of what you are, who you are, where you are.

The last line is the mind which is very huge and covers the world. It sees present life from beginningless ancient time, in which we know that we were there because we are here. It knows there are no gaps in life, which burns as a candle. Even if one burns out, the next one goes. In that way, in our life lineage, everyone is carried.

"I now fully avow." I admit the many, many sufferings which I, through my own body, speech, and mind, have caused. This repentance doesn't occur just once, or every day. Actually, in the deep center of our life, we are always checking it. If we don't check it, there is no tomorrow, no way to receive tomorrow. In other words, the entire system checks it, even as you rest and sleep. Your consciousness is utterly somewhere else, but your body is checking where to be, with whom to be. Saying it another way, the body is choosing the most level place to sleep, the most level place to sit. If you are tilted, in about an hour your body will start to feel the right place.

"All my ancient wrong actions arising from beginning-less greed, anger and delusion, based on mind, speech and body, all together I now fully avow."

Actually, when repentance, self-acknowledgement, is completed, all qualities of Buddha nature, all Precepts, are already accomplished in the existence of our avowal. The Ten Precepts, Three Pure Precepts, Triple Treasure Precepts, and Sange are actually all pointing to the same thing, or coming out from the same thing. What we see is all appearing in relative forms, and the mind is reflected in those relative forms. Each of those forms is actually how you can be. Our knowledge about what we are doing, what we are experiencing, is very, very small, but what is happening is incredibly complicated. The relation between the Precepts and the words of avowal is like a person who is always thankful, and is always able to say, "I'm sorry." It is the bright side of things and the shadowy side of things. The more you care for someone or something, the more you are afraid of them or it. Do you notice this? The more you are concerned deeply about some object, and get to know it, the more you feel, "This is getting hard for me."

My experience with zazen has the same kind of feeling. It was quite easy in the beginning, very tempting and very far away, so I put lots of energy into doing zazen. A deep excitement, I felt. Year after year that excitement faded away and zazen became like an enemy to conquer. Now I cannot do it without giving zazen deep respect. Physically, it is almost nothing, like brushing my teeth or going to bed, but it is hard to really let it arise and let me do it. I feel the same about the Precepts.

Chapter 24

Triple Treasure

"The Triple Treasure is an historical expression, in human language, which says, 'Come back...come back home.'"

Triple Treasure

Continually alert, and sometimes nervous, you think, "Am I doing alright? Is it alright to go this way?" When you totally admit you are as you are, and totally trust in being, this is Triple Return to Three Treasures: Buddha, Dharma, Sangha.

"Buddha, Dharma, Sangha" means "ultimate awakening, truth, all beings." To understand the Triple Treasure is very difficult. For example, we call the second one, "Dharma Treasure," "Essential Truth." We came from Truth, we are in Truth, and we will go back to Truth. It is almost impossible for each of us to observe the whole Truth. Although we trust the functioning of our whole body and mind, we still have to admit to the limitation of our sense organs, of our body and mind. Watching the ancient light from innumerable stars, we identify that as the present. Watching the ancient rock, we have countless ages beside us. Still, we pay little attention to the rock. Listening to sounds of insects flying around, we measure them as very short-lived creatures. Or standing by the aged, old trees, since our senses are very much related with the eternity of things, it feels good to stand beside them. Yet, we know all existences have an ending. I still don't know what comes after that ending, and the limitation of our knowing is very obvious.

The Three Treasures come to you as an objective image of the realm of the senses. I can find them within me. If you can find them within you, you have obtained what you are going to be, what you are going to rest in, because they are limitless. To have indestructible confidence in yourself as the Triple Treasure is your final recognition of receiving the Precepts. This self-acknowledgement we usually call repentance. It means an immediate change of behavior toward every single other existence. Your mind goes toward each existence, seeing it, not how you wish to see it, but how it really is. This is the power of repentance. Seeing yourself as an enormous, long life is what this repentance is.

My speaking to you is one body of Triple Treasure. Any single phenomenon, any single being, is a perfect realization of Triple Treasure. Perfect enlightenment, perfect awakening, undefiled truth, purest truth, or the original face of truth, and perfect unity, perfect liberation, perfect harmony in any single phenomenon, any moment, is basic Triple Treasure. It is a particle, such that the whole is the same as a particle.

Historically, Triple Treasure was Shakyamuni Buddha, his teaching, and his living space, within which many other people, many other existences, were aware of what was happening there. This is called the realized Triple Treasure, or the historical Triple Treasure. The maintained Triple Treasure, or the cultural Triple Treasure, like Buddha statues, or the cushion itself, comes in many forms. Many Tibetan tankas express the form of Dharma, and there are paintings, mandalas, music, cultural Dharma, and Sangha, too, in temples and churches. These are manifestations of Triple Treasure, abiding Triple Treasure, or expressed Triple Treasure. Behind or within these, there is the truth of Triple Treasure.

The Triple Treasure is an historical expression, in human language, which says, "Come back...come back home." When one returns to true self, one recognizes one has never been freaked out, it was just pretending, or something. One can present apparent selves in order to protect the true self and yet this true self is indestructible and eternal. It doesn't go through karma, but creates the shadow of karmic consciousness to let you know what is happening in history.

Seijo was a baby when her parents promised another family, who just had a boy, that they would marry in the future. When the children grew up, they wished to marry, but Seijo's parents changed their minds and decided she should marry a very wealthy man. Ochu, the boy, was very upset, and the night before the ceremony he stole her away with him. They lived far away, and had two children. After a while both of them began to miss their parents, so they returned, traveling down the Yang-tse River. Ochu left Seijo in the boat and went to see her parents, who told him that Seijo was sick in bed where she had been since he ran away from the village. Very surprised, Ochu went and got his wife and children, and brought them to see her parents. When Seijo walked into her bedroom, the sick woman stood up, like a dream walker, and walked toward the door. Right at the door they both smiled, and became one woman again. This is a koan: "Which one was the true Seijo?" Don't you experience this kind of thing all the time? It's like when you are feeling "off," and then the next moment you are "just right," and as soon as you say it, "Oh, wait a minute, I'm feeling a little bit blah, again."

When you return home, and enter your house, you become master of your home. Your home is your body. Returning to the self, the true self which is nobody, is nothing but the complete awakening. We call this Buddha.

Thinking about historical events and people's awareness about human life, we come to Shakyamuni Buddha's so-called "nirvana," or accomplishing the awakening. Different terminologies describe that occasion, the occasion of supreme understanding, finding the supreme way. Annuttara is "highest" or "largest," or "deepest," "nothing more than that." Samyaksambodhi means "right" or "complete enlightenment." At that moment all so-called Precepts are accomplished, although not in spoken words. "I and the great earth, all beings, at the same time accomplished the way," was spoken by Shakyamuni in the very first moment after his awakening. In the same awareness he saw that he wasn't the first one. He had to admit that there were many past Buddhas who accomplished the Way in the same way.

People who sit in zazen agree that the Buddha, to whom we offer full respect, is Shakyamuni Buddha. He was a human being. He spent half his life seeking Truth and taught about it the rest of his life. He said that he was not the first one to discover the Truth, that awakened people before him knew these things, how things are, what things consist of, how to manage our life. They were all very natural teachings. When I was in junior high school I had to write a complete list of the great people of the world and look into their biographies. I still remember how proud I was of how Shakyamuni Buddha lived naturally and died naturally. He died from a stomach problem, caused by a food offering. To the last moment he was with people, making sure that everyone was doing alright. Even then, he said, "Do not make me your idol after my death. Depend on yourselves as your own refuge." There are many examples of how clear he was, how ripened and refined a man he was.

Always, Buddha's teachings in Buddhist literature encourage us in our seeking of the Truth and our efforts to be our ideal self. Anyone can be the same as Buddha. This is again the continuous daily dilemma I am pointing out. We continually make mistakes and evaluate ourselves. If we do something sloppy, or utterly wrong, we cannot let it go. We get stuck in there and feel split. "I mustn't be like this," or "I'm actually not this bad." But each situation has lots of pitfalls, as you know. I keep stumbling into them, even if I am pretty good. Even to speak about it is embarrassing! "Maybe I'm basically a bad man? No good!" Maybe we are in a sort of helpless state. Looking around, we don't see any ideal image to follow. People in love have this kind of view continuously. You admire someone from far away who doesn't pay any attention to you. You feel this helpless state. Often we feel as emotional as a high school boy or girl, "Maybe I'll go off to the mountains and never come back!" Or, "I'll jump off from the moonlight cliff and fall down below to the water." But we have no courageous spirit to do it.

What kind of experience takes place when you experience that you are nobody but Buddha, yourself, that your entire mind and body is made of the same things as Buddha? Whatever you experience is all part of the true unity. Messy things are part of it. Going to the bathroom was part of Buddha's practice. When you get old there is no doubt that lots of your body is not working any more, like an old car, an old machine. That is also Buddha. And also part of Buddha is someone who cares for you. It's like the time when I got lost in the mountains and didn't get back to the Temple until after midnight. My mother and brother were waiting for me. A hot bath was ready, dinner and a warm bed were ready for me, a wet, hungry rat. I knew that there was no difference between Buddha's mind and my mother's mind. He was alive.

If you open your eyes to see the Buddha, Buddha is everywhere. If you open your eye to see the mind-world, world of mind is there. If you see only the material world, you have an eye to see it. If you observe the human beings' world, it becomes very chaotic, people suffering. Yet it is not necessary to suffer. Some artists do not suffer, just watch the eternal subject, carving out, writing down, the beauty of existence. That heavenly world exists. If you observe all beings as part of the process, reaching ultimate Buddhahood together, you see all as Bodhisattvas, coming from completion into the incomplete world. This process is called "Mahasattva, Great Being". Existences called Bodhisattvas strive for completion of ultimate perfection. They seek to trust the perfect process of life forms. Once in a while you sense this in your daily life. Arhats, saints, every single one of us, carries that spirit already, from childhood, seeking ultimate purity, desiring to express it in ultimate form among people, among all beings.

We call the whole teaching "Dharma." Usually this "Dharma" is very specific in its meaning as "right teaching," "right law," or "true law." The word, "dharma," expresses what it is: "Existence." It can mean either a phenomenal existence or noumenal existence. Whatever appears within you, without you, or with you, is called "dharma," but the original meaning of "dharma" is the thing which unites all elements, which brings things together, and maintains that which came together. When you are ordained, you are asked if you accept this. You answer, "I will," which means, "I'm aware of it and it will go on; awareness will be maintained." So we call it "Dharma."

In the past several centuries, in all scientific fields, even in technology, people have had so-called Dharma Eye. People of genius have devoted their entire effort to drawing out the truth of nature. Western scientists have worked on this a great deal. We can say that those people went into the Eye which sees the Law of Things, the Rule of Things, how things exist. This is called "Ho Gen," Dharma Eye. The Dharma Treasure includes all those many discoveries about life.

We know what "sangha" is, in a limited sense, but it takes our entire life to know what kind of Sangha has existed since ancient times. The whole history of living beings can be seen in the concrete forms of Sangha, the long history of kindness in ancient times. Maintaining the quality of life of the people in the sangha, safely and well, has been the basic concern. In modern life, you don't need to know the whole text of laws of the state, but you may read them and feel, "Oh, I am caught," or with a different attitude, you may think, "I am living in a big safe house." In the same way, the Precepts are working even if you don't study every line. When Mahayana Buddhism developed in India, people called themselves Bodhisattva Mahasattvas, and they called their communities ghana. Instead of saying "sangha" they called themselves "So-and-so Ghana." Some called themselves "So-and-so Gate," for going in and out. Some called themselves "So-and so Wind or Force." Sometimes Sanghas are called "mountain." Climb up and climb down. Some are called "So-and-so Ha." "Ha" is tide. These poetic names came to be known as schools or sects, in Eastern terminology.

There are many stages to understanding Sangha. You can understand it as the appearance of religious views, or as a response to the needs of the whole society. For Buddha, Sangha means the whole of existence, with no distinction between Buddha's existence and things' existences. Various reasons bring people together. They may gather because of fear, or because they feel they lack something. Maybe there is some benefit, maybe no benefit. We see all sorts of social structures, in business, school, hospitals, and religious orders. Sometimes you may think, "There are things I have to do at home," and you hesitate to join in. But you are surrounded, and when the train comes you finally say, "I have to go because everyone is going." But even if you decide not to get on the train, you are still part of the Sangha.

There are many reasons why people come together. If you put sugar on the ground, in one hour you see that ants are gathering. If Buddha appears it makes one "sangha." When one hundred people come, there is still one sangha. What sangha means is to really know what is harmony of life, what is peace of life, what is freedom. Instinctively humans and living things try this sangha, for instance, even in marriage. Maintenance of life is the best function of sangha.

In the Precepts Ceremony, we talk about the Return to the Triple Treasure:

Return to Buddha
Return to Dharma
Return to Sangha.

In China and Japan it is called:

Namu kie butsu
Namu kie ho
Namu Kie so.

"Ki" is "return," not returning something to somebody, but you return. And "e" is "to," "return to." Usually "e" is "depending on," maybe fully depending on, like putting your thumb out to hitch a ride from someone. At that time you are "e," depending on whomever stops. You don't tell them, "I must go to Fresno." Instead, you completely rely upon that person. You become a relaxed passenger. Getting on a ferry, if you worry, "This boat looks so old, maybe it will have water coming up," that's not it. You completely give in. That is the meaning of "e." It is a very deep sensation.

"Kie" is saranam in Sanskrit, or "homage," something to do with home. There are many English translations, and it means "to go into, jump into, plunge into." Where you plunge into is actually where you have started. So you can imagine you are born and take a journey and go all the way around the world and come back to the starting point. Coming back, returning to where you started, it is already gone. So you ask "What was it?" That is saranam gacchami. Gacchami means "go." Or if you are waiting for a person to come back, gacchami means "coming in." You do both, like a little kid lost in the village, you finally come back to your parents and jump into this big valley. That is what "kie" is.

Chapter 25

Three Pure Precepts and the Prohibitory Precepts

"It is when we are attempting very sincere, very serious communication, a Precept reveals itself."

Three Pure Precepts

We call the Three Pure Precepts:

Sho butsu gi kai
Sho Zen ho kai
Sho shu gyo kai.

All three, together, mean "embracing all existences." They are about how to include all existence within your life, how to sustain all good, while quitting all kinds of wrong actions. The third one is embracing and sustaining all and every being. These three are a precise description of the contents of awakening, what was contained in Buddha's mind. In English, we say,

First, to embrace and sustain right conduct.
Second, to embrace and sustain every good.
Third, to embrace and sustain all beings.

In the meal sutra we hold up the bowl with the spoon in it and bow. The first bite is for stopping all evil deeds, second bite is for doing all good, third bite is to save all existences. Finally we say, "all together accomplish the Buddha Way," and start to eat.

Prohibitory Precepts

The Triple Treasure and Three Pure Precepts are actually not describing different things. They are the same thing from different angles and depths. The Ten Grave Precepts have to be seen in many ways, and we can ask why people's understandings of them were written down. The answer is the same as why you send a signal to others, especially since after you have kept one week or one month of silent practice, you begin to sense what a big mess you have made by talking. Often you are not aware of how powerful your words are, but then you are bound by them. It's like you dig a hole and then you're in it, a pretty deep hole. If you are an expert in negation, like a nihilist or critic, it's like words are peeling off part of yourself, exposing yourself among people, so finally nothing is left. Or maybe you are cutting away your foundation so you get very high, and discover that you are spaced out, have no contact with anything.

So why are there the words of Precepts? We also have the Ten Commandments of Moses and Jesus, which have mystical elements, very penetrating compassion, carrying words, like searchlights, into darkness, for people to see who they are and find a path. When dangerous times come, religious consciousness becomes very powerful, to protect life, itself. This is a very instinctive and intuitive ability of human beings.

The Ten Grave Precepts were brought by Bodhidharma from India to China. Before they became ten, there were hundreds of rules of order for Buddhist life. These ten are like ten beads of light, coming from the center and taking different textures and colors, and if they become very radiant, they appear as one white light. Bodhidharma called it One-Mind. "I shing kai tai." "One mind, Precepts body." He did not mean just this one mind, but entire mind, entire life. These are the Ten Precepts. Zazen is to actualize that Buddha mind immediately. It doesn't matter whether you realize it or not. Bodily participation in zazen, itself, is the proof. Zazen is the concrete form of the utter belief in who you are, and there is no thinking about it, or about anything. Humankind and every single thing lives and exists fully in their best way. We may observe, and see the growth process, but if we are within it, we don't see that process. Every moment is the completion of practice.

Our expression of the Precepts is a very high discipline. It goes beyond nations, races, and differences of sex. Thus, we have, "no killing, no stealing, no illusory talk, no blame, no praise," and the others. These written Precepts are the expression of Buddha nature, our true nature. They are not demands "to do, not to do," or "should do." It is natural to follow this high discipline. It is Buddha's way of life.

I would like to introduce how Bodhidharma expressed right understanding of the Precepts: He said, "To receive is to transmit. To transmit is to be awakened. Thus, to be awakened in Buddha mind is called 'true receiving of Precepts.'" This "Buddha mind" is what you call "Buddha nature," or your true nature, the truth of your existence. The first line of each of Bodhidharma's Precepts is, "Self nature is mysteriously profound." He meant that the truth of your existence is so delicate, so precious, so mysterious and wondrous, it is hard to know. No one can understand it, but it is occuring constantly, in front of you. Usually we say "my life," meaning the fifty or seventy years we have lived, in which one may feel "I didn't accomplish anything," or, "It had no meaning." Maybe you think, "I do not understand my life." It's hard to perceive the whole figure of your life.

Going through the Precepts, I feel that it is kind of like kneading emptiness in your hand. Like pizza dough, or you are making a cake, many different kinds and shapes of cake. The Indian Buddhists had 250 precepts for monks and another 100 for nuns. The essence of each Precept, whether there are ten, forty-eight, or a thousand Precepts, is in each a very great effort to express something of what we are. These Precepts are our actual basic functioning, the functioning of our awareness. Being aware of them, whatever occurs, we know that dualistic or changing dimensions of thinking, even emotional reactions to things, are all tentative. Even if we accept these reactions, we trust that the truth within us is not twisted. Even when you see the suffering and helplessness of others, still you trust that they are basically fine and strong enough to go through their problem.

When you say to yourself, "This feels right, so I will do it," you are not relying on how something looks. Sometimes you think, "That looks fine but something is wrong." Awareness of the Precepts provides a pretty straightforward standard. If someone blames you for something, and you are doing right and fine, the blaming is like a cool wind. But if you start to get confused and wonder, "Did I do something wrong?" you feel the blame before it comes. The knowledge came to you already, from outside or inside.

Whether we exist alone or among all, these Precepts express extremely kind concern, letting us know what truth is. Even though it remains the fate of language that it cannot fully reach to what is being expressed in words, the Precepts are a clear and pervasive expression looking toward the future, toward all directions, even toward the past, shining a bright light which reveals things are they are. If we do not pay full attention to people, to ourselves, to things, then the light of the Precepts is pretty weak. It is when we are attempting very sincere, very serious communication, a Precept reveals itself. In this way your true face reveals itself, without defending or covering up with something else. Thus you are revealed as an extremely honest being, bare-minded, powerfully realizing the Precepts. This happens both by your instinct and your intuition.

Chapter 26

No Killing Life, No Stealing, No Attaching to Fulfillment

"Shikantaza is one immediate answer to the question of what life is all about, and getting up from shikantaza is a continuous answer to how you live."

First Precept: No Killing Life

Self nature is mysteriously profound.
In the midst of eternal dharma, not to
give rise to the view of stopping and
extinction is called

'No Killing Life Precept.'

When you say, "life" there are various lives you may see, but if you are looking at your own life, you feel what it is, but you can't explain. You have to describe various events and what happened. So many times we say "I" or "my" or "mine." There is something going on which makes it possible to say so. So when I pay attention to this "I" it is always the true self, in all attempts to express something. Even misspeech points to the truth. Even very confused talk points to what is to be spoken. It is just the expression which wasn't clear, because the reality of the "I" was many elements existing in confusion.

Imagine a very tough, strong, vigorous cowboy holding a gun, in a showdown. The other cowboy misses his shot, and this cowboy now has another chance to control everything, but he is waiting to shoot. We see he can kill. What is going on in his mind? If he gets into a philosophical discussion with himself, he has lost his chance. If he throws away the gun you see what is in his mind. He cannot kill. That is our true nature. And yet, for survival, we have to take many lives, and we always get into this dilemma. Eating vegetables or fish is basically the same dilemma. What is it that is living? Precepts exist to cause a dilemma for us, and a deeper understanding of what this giving/taking life is.

Over one hundred thousand million years of sustaining our life, each of our lives, we, naturally, have had to take the lives of others. It is a daily thing we do, to sustain our life and continue to live. For all of us, this first Precept, "No killing life," is a kind of impossible Precept to keep. It was first spoken a long time ago, about twenty-six centuries, and people, living together, vowed to keep this Precept. Now it is the twentieth century and we are still living our life in a very primitive way. We are facing the great danger of the decay of all lives on earth, not only humankind.

If we take this Precept literally, the only way to keep it is to die without food. It sets forth a contradiction. Even if we don't directly participate in killing lives, if somebody else takes a life so we can survive, it is the same thing. So Precepts are not just about your ethical conduct. They have something to do with yours' and others' basic nature. Bodhidharma taught, "When you do not give rise to the idea of birth and extinction, this is called 'No Killing Life.'" ' "Truth of eternity," "jo ju ho." "Jo ju" is "eternal dwelling." "Ho" is "truth." This Precept is about giving birth to "no birth/no extinction."

Dogen Zenji expresses this Precept, "Do not kill. Do not let other people kill. Beyond that, flourish our Buddha seeds." He covers the ethics of our life and the deeper meaning, what this life is all about. We eat living food. Through our food we learn constantly how to live on this earth. We are constantly supported by all phenomenal currents of life; we are lived by all beings. That is the truth. We are lived by whom and whatever we take, by their teachings that guide us. One way to live is to show all of their natures through our existence. It is different from our usual way of continuously exploring our capacities for what we really want to do.

"Jo" relates to wellbeing, and satisfaction of our desires, all kinds of desires. It feels like one desire leads to another desire, and it keeps going on and on. Endlessly we do things because of the wishes and desires that arise within us. Is this the only way to live? One hundred thousand million lives came into our life, which is each of these dynamic lives, and we are fulfilling their wish of who they wanted to be. That is the way to live the Precepts. We listen to all existences, how every being wanted to be, not only what we ate, what we took, but all existences. Continuous existence is in each moment of our life. Whether you are being aware of your deeds or not it is happening in that way. It is like eating a meal, our body is big and the food is little, so we say, "I took this life." But when you compare the amount of food you took and the amount of energy of your life, they are actually the same. This is a very interesting way to keep one moment of the universe. All beings offer their life for it and return to nothing. All beings return to nothing, offering their lives and making one moment possible. This is how we humans live, how vegetables live and die. The farmer's job is to take care of the vegetables, maybe to sprinkle the water. Maybe the vegetables will say, "I'm sorry, I'm eating you." Maybe only humans say, "I killed this lettuce." So practice and life become the same thing. The question of how you are going to live is answered by expressing, not just understanding, what life is all about.

Shikantaza is one immediate answer to the question of what life is all about, and getting up from shikantaza is a continuous answer to how you live. How you live is how everything lives. For this reason, one period of sitting is not something we do as an exercise to reach to some kind of enlightened state. We all know this world is the radiant dynamic of the enlightened world, enlightened functioning. There is no need to seek after enlightenment. The functioning of each sense organ is part of the experiencing of enlightenment. Every second many, many elements of enlightenment are happening. Life was born as awakened existence.

Humankind experienced the Second World War. Since then there have been many wars and battles and still we hear that the fire is growing. It is extinguished in one place and moves to another. This is a continuous sign of a sickness we have. In any case, we must not cause the Third World War. To create a peaceful world, the ultimate answer is to sit together. We don't know who will come to sit next to us, mother or lover or stranger, we cannot know beforehand. But sitting together, for a couple of minutes or maybe days, gradually lets us understand. Sitting together lets us see things without argument or fight, because the body is being taught to understand what this body, this life, is, and how other lives are existing.

Second Precept: No Stealing

> Self nature is mysteriously profound.
> Unattainable dharma. Not to raise mind
> of attainable is called
>
> 'No stealing or robbing'."

It is obvious, when you take something that does not belong to you, or is not given to you, you get in trouble. This is a limited meaning of "no stealing." To understand the broader meaning of this Precept, think about your existence before you existed, and after you will finish existing. In between, we have this issue of "no stealing." The subject opens up, in a very big way, the question of whether our practice and behavior is encouraging life as one identity. In other words, do we "possess"? In ancient times all Buddhists, monks and nuns, and lay people, gave up possessions, to experience a deeper understanding about life. There are many ways to exist. Some people are relatively wealthy, some have a difficult time surrounding themselves with things, and some have no things to take care of. Some want to be satisfied with pleasure, as much as they can find, for as long as it lasts.

To have a human body on this earth is a complete contradiction. We cannot escape from it and it is a hard phenomenon to see through. It has been said that Truth is so profound it is hard to observe it thoroughly. In every moment each thing's existence is interdepending, beyond our understanding. Sense organs cannot reach to the depths of the Truth, and yet every day we discover we are still here. As you become aware of yourself, you desire clothes that fit you, nobody but you. Your house, city, country are familiar, or at least the unquestionably familiar dynamics of your body are realized there. If you are in a totally strange place, unable to understand others, you begin to understand what a different world you have created. Where you are becomes what you are. Independent interdependency is there as one personality.

The basic recognition of this Precept contains the dilemma of possessing everything and anything, and possessing nothing. This is the human contradiction. The more wealth you have, the more effort you need to take care of it. On the other hand, the fewer possessions you have, the more you are free. One day it all pops, and you begin to feel, "I am going to die now." What was this life? "Running around." It all becomes a very pale memory. Dying people show a very noble face. They have realized the truth of existence. They suffer and suffer with lots of pain in their bodies and many ideas. Finally, they give up everything. Something heavy drops off, everything drops off, and their faces become very relieved, relieved from suffering, and very noble in appearance.

Zazen practitioners are people who go through that kind of experience very often while they are still quite young. They return to life, not in the same place, same time, but very far advanced, with very deep concern about things medicine, meal bowls, clothing, food. They know all of these things are transient materials, so they share them. Buddha's order was like that.

Our study is to look into the real meaning, the true meaning, of "no stealing." The ordinary meaning of stealing is to take something from others, make others' thing your own. Together with this meaning, we can observe what the whole thing is about. Something happened, and we appeared on this earth as a very small drop of life, which grew up as matter. A little circle of energy appeared in your mother's circle of energy, and when the time came, it started to separate. It looks like two, but, as you know, mother and child cannot be separated. Even if the mother passes away, that mother is the mother of this child, always. Yet we think this human being is an individual existence. Because this human shape is dynamic, and moves among many things, we do not question that it has a separate existence.

It is necessary to find which way you are going to move on this earth, what kind of life you want to create. Eventually we begin to understand that we are truly an individual existence. This individual existence is a universal thing, in itself. A life of activity becomes a creative art form for you. So study becomes important, research becomes important, also communication. All are necessary. Yet this individual existence is inseparable from this universe.

Please remember this "no stealing" Precept. It is the ultimate recognition that you have nothing to lose. Even if you, your whole body, is stolen by somebody, your whole mind by somebody, you have not lost anything. One example is devotion, which is to give yourself to a person or situation. The devotional relationship of teacher and disciple is not one sided. To have two bodies is at this point a remarkable sign of freedom. Mind has utterly become one, yet you liberate each other. This is the deep relationship of real friends, mother and child, father and child, wife and husband, friends.

Having something stolen is a little comical. Giving something is another side of it. We feel very good when we give something to others. The more pure it is, the more tasteless it is. The more content it has, emotions, sensations between yourself and others, the heavier the experience you go through when you give something and the more you don't forget what you have given. You may still not forget it after ten years, if it's a very big present, but if you forget the next day, that's very nice. The best way to give a present to others is to give the work you do. You can forget it immediately because attachment doesn't follow it.

Third Precept: No Attaching to Fulfillment

Self nature is mysteriously profound.
Truth of no attachment. Not to give
birth to attaching to loving is called

'no desiring', 'fu in yoku', 'no wrong, no
scattered desiring'.

It always puzzles us what this truly means. Is this only for married or engaged couples? Or is it just the subject of men and women? For most people, this Precept has been limited to "No committing adultery."

This, "No committing adultery" is very interesting. Bodhidharma spoke of many projected desires. He explained it this way: "Not to give birth to attachment in the truth of nonattachment." It is called, "No desire for fulfillment." Attachment is, absolutely, illusion, at this point. At one time this was a very big subject for me, especially until my marriage day. For me, to touch a woman was a very big fear. It always caused deep guilt within me. It was a sort of strange experience. I am wondering what it was, what caused that deep anxiety, which appeared as guilt, or maybe helpless regret. Before I knew any woman, I was talking about purity of monkhood. My mother was very concerned about my fixed ideas. You women may be familar with this kind of feeling. You may have feared man in many ways, wanting to keep your own purity. The difference between pure and impure you didn't know, but you wanted to be a single existence and become a nun in a very holy, unstained existence. You still have a deep curiosity and a sort of respect for people who lead a single life, don't you?

It is only in very recent times that I really notice the difference between purity of love, and attachment, and I'm very much aware of my attachment in love. One is attached to parts of the whole thing. I really understand, now, why Bodhidharma said, "Not to give birth to attachment, in the truth of nonattachment." Nonattachment is truth. To be fond of things, particularly your favorite things, is what attachment means. In such situations, we give birth to attachment. "I like this, I don't like this." But when we begin to sense why we like this and don't like that, it becomes very complicated. Sometimes unlike and dislike go together. Sometimes alike and dislike go together, that is, if you see somebody who is very much like you, you dislike that person. This sticking to each other or rejecting each other is very hard because intellect doesn't help, and emotion is no way to solve it.

This seems to be a much deeper subject than what we can understand and manage. If somebody appears while we have a very peaceful married life, this person may appear attractive to you. In this life there are these kinds of absurd experiences and puzzles about who you are, causing problems. These ancient emotions involve lots of jealousy and fantasy. It seems that you have to go through this process, get over it, and get to a more transparent stage of understanding what you are and what others are.

There is only you and Absolute Being, so there is basic confusion in having two objects as the Absolute. Yet, the ethical meaning of this Precept is quite obvious. Adultery is a confused state. It causes separation from relating with whom you really wish to relate. That is a kind of chasing after many rabbits and not being able to catch one. The basic problem is not objective, but, rather, subjective. The Absolute has many symbolic forms and images, which actually represent what you were born as, and whom you are serving. The Absolute is this one, it is who we are. This is why we keep following the life of no identity, in order to cleanse our life. It is continually important to have an appreciation for who and what formed you, which is watching your life.

This Precept also relates to the choice of whether to go to one teacher or another teacher. From childhood, we have many teachers. In Japan we have all kinds of teachers. The final teacher is called Dharma Master, or Basic Master. This teacher confirms your completion of practice, liberates you from him or her, and lets you be an independent existence, deciding everything by yourself, taking all responsibility for what you do.

In university I had several fine teachers. Sokuo Eto was a sort of theologian about zazen. He clarified why Dogen Zenji has been considered the basic founder of zazen in Japan. He discussed previous masters, and the difference between Rujing, the last Chinese master of the Soto lineage, and Dogen's way. Professor Sokuo Eto passed away when I was in school. I owe him very much personally, and also in my study of Buddhism. Having so many teachers felt to me like some sort of adultery, in a much deeper sense. I was very thirsty to learn, and each master, each teacher, fulfilled me. Finally, my Dharma Master settled me down, "No more seeking!" It was a sort of peak experience for me not to look around any more. I have been feeling these days how he felt when I went away from him and continued to practice with more scholars. Yet it always feels very peaceful whenever I feel these masters are present in zazen practice. No more questions, and continuous support always, from right behind me. This support, this presence, for me, is absolute. The one who is right here I cannot see. I can only feel. The ones who I see in front of me, all are his manifestation. I mean the Master's continuity is right here. I can see it. Right here. For always, in all ways, he comes to me.

Chapter 27

No Illusory Words, No Selling the Wine of Delusion, No Dwelling on Past Mistakes, No Praise or Blame, No Hoarding Materials or Teachings

"Every minute, every second, we are unfolding teachings, and the materials are the dynamics of life"

Fourth Precept: No Illusory Words

Self nature is mysteriously profound.
Unexplainable dharma. Not to preach
one word is called

'no illusory words'.

What is unreal and what is real is a very big subject for all of us. The life we live feels fantastic, but it feels like a continuous dream. Our experiences of the past twenty years, forty years, even seventy years, where are they? It feels like all are embedded in the present moment and the dynamic life we live. When we look into our past, the words we have spoken to ourselves and others show a narrow perspective. Even if we make our best effort not to lie, not to speak untruth, still we feel we have many times spoken illusory words. We are afraid we might still be doing this, and that this must still be going on.

It is very difficult to describe an actual thing in language. The word, "cat" is the word, "cat." That word cannot become the cat, it merely points to something. If we can experience something together with another person, we do not need so many words. But communication can be complicated. When I say "zafu" all of us understand it, but for people who don't know that a zafu is a black cushion, "zafu" is just a sound. Also, "zafu" doesn't point to something we don't know, but that invisible realm is important when we discuss communication.

Intentionally telling a lie is obviously a useless thing to do, and yet we do it once in awhile if we are caught up in some difficult situation. We lie, tentatively, and then we get into more problems. Sometimes it is to protect ourselves, or to save ourselves, or to relieve other people from difficulty. Very complicated emotions go along with it. We all know that kind of situation, but the lack of clear recognition that you lied has to be corrected. It has to be worked out.

Fifth Precept: No Selling the Wine of Delusion

> Self nature is mysteriously profound.
> Truth of original basic purity. Not to
> give birth of ignorance is called 'no
> selling wine, no drinking wine'.

We try not to intoxicate our body and mind, because if we go along with the heavy trip of intoxication, a very powerful life, or chemical, takes over our life. We don't know what was eaten, what was taken, or what was given. The unity of energy with other existences is very delicate, and if we are intoxicated, we lose the opportunity to unite with them. In a sense, nothing is wrong to do. Right and wrong are just our way of perceiving things and evaluating how human life can be, either in good shape or very dangerous shape. Our body decides what to do about bodily intoxication, but our mind is open to enormous amounts of teaching, of many kinds. Those teachings work powerfully with the mind. So to delude the true nature is what we call "intoxication." Hopefully, we will observe our whole life with Buddha's body and mind, and live through this life without much delusion. Once we give our lives to delusion, we lose contact with many important things and people. Keep your mind clear and let it penetrate through things and all people and situations. That is why the Precepts are offered. They are not just to prohibit you from doing one thing or another, but to keep your true nature functioning at its best.

This Precept can literally refer to wine, as well as other things which intoxicate our body and mind. This desire for intoxication has lasted for centuries and centuries, and the more heavily we get into illusion or delusion, the more removed we are from ourselves. Bodhidharma says that self-nature, our true nature, is a fantastic thing, and yet illusions and delusions take over and cover up our true nature. Then we are helpless. We cannot recover by ourselves. The powerful forces of love, compassion, and extreme clarity of mind, which let a dynamic body be in the right place at the right time, aren't easy to sustain, especially when we intoxicate ourselves over and over again and spoil ourselves. So these words, "No selling the wine of delusion," are kind words.

There are many stories about uncontrolled, helpless situations caused by the powerful effects of intoxication on our delicate bodies and miinds. You drink strong wine and step on an insect, unaware. In the next life you will be born as that insect, and then you will be stepped on by a drunken man. If you wish to control or conduct yourself well, the only way is by inner recognition of yourself. At first, curiosity about intoxication and the relatively gentle effect of intoxication washes over you. If it becomes a habit, you don't know whether it is you intoxicating the wine or the wine intoxicating you. It becomes a continuous, ongoing relationship. Using heavy liquor is like taking a lot of sugar, continuously causing you to be sick. Eating rich food all the time makes you diabetic. Strong wine or whiskey makes your brain fogged and doesn't let your brain recover. Smoking is the same, and there is also a powerful mind reaction to marijuana. I had one terrible experience. I thought I could sit in zazen after drinking quite a lot of sake, and it was terrible. The body is like a boneless creature if you drink too much. You cannot even walk straight. If you have no control over intoxication it is best to give it a vacation. Refrain from that state for two or three days and see how the body feels. It is important to develop your experience of the cleansing sensation.

Even a so-called religious way can be the wine of delusion. Many times we call on spiritual subjects in order to polish ourselves, but these can have the same kind of effect as wine.

When some religion causes you to become excited, bringing you to a state of ecstatic excitement, you'd better think that this isn't the ultimate. Yet there are many religions which focus on an ultimate state. If zazen practice makes you feel like that, your zazen is not the right one. An intoxicated, agitated state is the opposite from great wisdom, opposite from a clear perspective on what this existence, this life, is all about. Great wisdom is something which makes you want to deeply appreciate yourself and others. If practice causes that deep appreciation and respect, there is peace and satisfaction. That is what real religion does. Then one has perfect contact with the self, with the ultimate.

Sixth Precept: No Dwelling on Past Mistakes

> Self nature is mysteriously profound. In the midst of unmistakable truth, not to speak of past mistakes is called the Precept of
>
> 'no speaking of past mistakes'.

The Sixth and Seventh Precepts relate with the Fourth Precept, "No illusory words." So there is no speaking of people's mistakes and misunderstandings, no praising yourself while you are feeling blame of others, and no praising others while you are blaming yourself. The spirit of this is thinking before speaking or acting, and, instead, offering good actions, thoughts, and speech. These Precepts are about words, the many sides of language. It is important to speak with fine timing and with truth from within. The true loving quality which appears with words is necessary if we wish to relate with other people.

Seventh Precept: No Praise or Blame

> Self nature is mysteriously profound. In
> the midst of equality, in the midst of
> identical dharma, identity of truth, no
> speaking of self and others is called the
> Precept of
>
> 'no praise or blame'.

The Seventh Precept speaks of comparing, "I am better than them," or, "I am not so good as him." This comparative sense makes many problems. Once it arises, it inexhaustibly continues because it is a relative concept and has no place to rest. It always moves. It gives no satisfaction. Even one who has become the most famous man in the world is still afraid, "Someone will become more famous than me." Right behind love of fame there is a shame, too. This is how the comparative sense works. To go beyond this sense or mind attitude is what this Seventh Precept is pointing to.

Like a scale, always the mind acts to put yourself high and others low. In Buddha mind there is no such activity. The scale is always level. There are no others. There is no self. Others are self and self is others, so comparing weights is impossible. Every Buddha and every ancestor realizes that he is the same as the limitless sky. When every Buddha Patriarch realizes that he is the whole sky and whole great earth, when he appears with a great body, there is no inside or outside. If he appears as a true body, there is no soil on the earth. It means he is the earth itself.

Dogen Zenji said there is no being proud of yourself and devaluing others, because there are no such others to devalue. When you devalue others, you are scratching at your body. When you are proud of yourself, you are scratching at the air.

Eighth Precept: No Hoarding Materials or Teachings

> Self nature is mysteriously profound. In
> the midst of all-pervading truth, not to
> raise hoarding, attaching on any single
> form, is called
>
> 'no hoarding' Precept.

Dogen Zenji's words on the Eighth Precept were:

"One phrase, one force, myriad phenomena. One Truth, one confirmation, All Buddha, All Patriarch. It has never been hoarded at all."

When you understand that everything was given to everyone in the beginning, a sense comes that there is nothing to limit this as "mine" and that as "not mine." When you go to the mountain and see a flower blooming, and you pick it up, break it, and make it yours. This is attachment. If you let it be there for everything and everyone, this is what "no attachment" is. The original meaning is two characters, "stingy" and "greedy." I might think, "This is mine and that is yours. The whole thing was given to me so you cannot take it from me." If you keep something, you may have had the idea that it was possessed by you, but it was not possessed by you. You become very poor by having this idea. Dogen Zenji said, "When you open your hand, everything is in your hand. When you close your hand, the air is very limited." Explaining this idea of possession in this very pure way, naturally you understand this Precept.

When I say, "Everything is given to you," it sounds like everything belongs to you, and you may feel really good. But when I say, "Nothing belongs to you," you may feel bad. Even yourself doesn't belong to you! You are everything. This means you actually have no self to limit. Knowing this Precept is having this deep understanding. Every single thing we appreciate is all public truth and whole Dharma. Teaching is, maybe, the unseen, or spiritual, part of Truth, and the material, or visible, part is public Truth. Even if a child dies after one week, you cannot say she didn't have the whole thing. Maybe you put your idea on this occasion, but she may say, "No, I lived enough." Every minute, every second, we are unfolding teachings, and all materials are the dynamics of life. So there is nothing to hoard, nothing to not show to people, nothing to keep apart from the whole, calling it your own.

And yet, in ordinary life we have a dilemma. When someone asks us to help some group, or themselves, how do we respond? We seem to see very unhappy situations in the external world, reflecting different circumstances. Political movements put forth methods to solve social problems, and sometimes you offer your energy, hoping to solve a basic problem. But something is missing when we act in that way. We are forgetting something. We do not know the reason for their suffering. It could be a national policy which is wrong, but this approach is a seesaw game. When you press very hard on one side of the argument, you see just half of the situation. If you press the other side, it looks like the right answer is over there. The necessity of acting becomes a big challenge. What to do, right now? This is the basic matter. You don't have to start something new. You just live on, go on living.

Chapter 28

No Being Angry, No Abusing the Triple Treasure

"Let your hand touch the water. Maybe try a few exercises. Then you swim, and get to know what it is, instead of walking around the pool and discussing the philosophy of swimming, day after day."

Ninth Precept: No Being Angry

> Self nature is mysteriously profound. In
> the midst of selfless truth, truth of
> selflessness, no measuring of oneself is
> called Precept of
> 'no being angry'.

Usually this Precept is kindly explained: "Disciple of the Buddha abstains from harboring hatred, malice, or ill will." This realm is very big, from very gentle anger to very developed rage, to the joy of hurting people. Anger changes from protective, to attacking, from negative to very positive. If there is just one person in the world, he will always be neutral. If someone is very angry but is the only person in the world, he is a little crazy. When you get mad at yourself, that means you're mad at another self. Maybe you turn your face and see yourself. Or you see yourself as other. This is very hard. Even if you are alone, this Precept applies, in the sense of self-hatred, self-deceiving, self-clinging.

If you become angry, you don't stop being Buddha. Anger appears, that's all. At that time you don't say to yourself that you shouldn't be getting angry. When you get close to fire, you don't say, "It should be cold!" Self-pride is another side of this phenomenon. Illusion causes a sensation, so it seems real. If you become wealthy and then look at the poor and feel pride, it is, at best, an unnecessary thing to experience. But we sometimes experience it that way. Or if you fail an examination, you feel depressed, which is natural, but it is notnecessary to stick on it for a long time. Making a judgment about yourself can be dangerous because you cover up reality. But putting up an idea that you should not be angry, you are covering reality. To turn the contents of anger into wisdom, you live it and learn something from it.

Anger is suffering, as you know. When someone gets very angry with you, his suffering is deeply concerned with you. He is letting you know how he exists. When he sees that you understand him, this anger disappears. When you see someone who is quite angry, when you really listen to him and completely understand his position, you, yourself, become angry. But, fortunately, anger does not stay. If you enjoy keeping it always, it will continue. But, otherwise, it is always slipping off of you. Anger causes life to shorten, which is the very opposite from self-nature, our eternal being, which has been the same, up to now, from its very origin, a pretty long time. To be here as a human being is a natural arrangement. But how rare it is. It is a miraculously rare thing, so we have utmost respect and care for our own life. For we are radiant life.

Tenth Precept: No Abusing the Triple Treasure - Buddha, Dharma, Sangha

Self nature is mysteriously profound. In
the midst of one Dharma, in the midst of
one great truth, not to give rise of mind
of sentient being or Buddha being is
called Precept of
'no abusing the Three Treasures'.

Why do we call them "treasures?" Buddha is Anuttarasamyaksambodhi, supreme, complete awakening, itself. Dharma is Truth, itself, which has never been stained. There is no way to stain it. Sangha is the entire contents of supreme awakening, the harmonious manifestation of Truth in form. Usually, we limit our understanding of the Triple Treasure to the functioning of the whole Sangha in the basic disciplines and teachings of practice, observed as Dharma, with members who wholeheartedly participate in that living situation, called Buddhas.

The ground of the deeper meaning of Triple Treasure is shikantaza. Bodhidharma speaks of this "No abusing the Triple Treasure" as understanding that our essence of existence, continuous awakening, is nothing but our basic nature. He teaches that self-nature is profound, contained in one Truth. Not to give birth to the dualistic observation that you and Buddha are different existences, not to give birth to dualistic thinking about sentient beings and Buddha, that is called "No abusing Triple Treasure."

To think of the Triple Treasure somewhere outside of you is the beginning of abusing, departing, from it. You are keeping yourself from it. If you understand Buddha and sentient beings as different beings, you are misunderstanding Triple Treasure and making the biggest mistake. You are cutting the Buddha's body and looking at his blood running.

What Sangha means is really knowing the harmony of life, the peace of living, the freedom of life. It is a very interesting thing to feel, really feel, how others are living. When you meet one little being, it might be a mosquito, or pine tree, or rock, to become Buddha with each of them is your practice. Do you understand? You become Buddha with each of them. This is communicating with a being that appeared for you, to make sure you are enlightened. It is also enlightened. This is how everything is actually happening but sometimes neither one knows what is going on. Sometimes both completely know what is going on.

If you believe in yourself as the creation of the absolute existence, whose presence is the only presence, then no problem. There is no separation between creator, creation, and created thing. You simply admit that you are an extension of the creation, a part of it, accepted by it. Eventually the effort becomes how to live within the intention of the creator. To find this out and follow this Way, is to live.

For each newborn person this learning has to be done, all over again. Maybe polishing of your own individuality has to be done all over again. A new generation cannot depend on parents or grandparents to be their utter support, so each individual has to start way-seeking all over again. Learning a language, how to hold a fork and knife, everything, we have to learn all over again.

Conditioning and ordinary common sense tell us that we are not enlightened, so we think that, first, we have to practice to become enlightened. The Soto tradition denies this and introduces zazen as the perfected action, the goal of practice. This is Dogen Zenji's view: People know that shikantaza is Buddha Dharma, but rarely do people understand this. From the very beginning, utter belief that you are Buddha, is required. You do not need to think about it, just do it. It's like a swimming teacher pushing you in the water, but the push is not necessary. First you try it. Let your hand touch the water. Maybe try a few exercises. Then you swim, and get to know what it is, instead of walking around the pool and discussing the philosophy of swimming, day after day.

When we study the Precepts we are studying our life in a very clear way. You come to it with an empty mind. But sometimes it is better not to study too much. If we have just a little blink of Precepts, you can develop them alone, because the whole thing is within you. I have said that it feels like there is just one great, limitless Precept, at the very center of my being. If I cannot sense it, I'm always away from it. At that time it feels like I am messing up my life as well as the life of others. Then I get more and more shy, especially when someone requests dokusan. It feels like I am in an extremely fancy and advanced university, where people are all professors, while I am the only student. If someone does not appear at dokusan time, because of traffic or sudden stomach ache or something, I feel that I'm saved. It's a very shaky life, Not to mess up is pretty hard practice....

GLOSSARY

AVIDYA
A Sanskrit word whose literal meaning is "ignorance", "delusion", "unlearned", "unwise" and opposite of "vidya"

BODHICITTA
A mind (including thought, action, feeling and speech) totally dedicated to others and to achieving full enlightenment in order to benefit all sentient beings as fully as possible

BODHISATTVA
An enlightened being who has put off entering paradise in order to help others attain enlightenment

BUDDHA
Awakened one, enlightened one

BUDDHA NATURE
The fundamental nature of all existences, which is already enlightened

BUDDHADHARMA
The way of the Buddha. It is his gift to sentient beings, reflecting the path he discovered after his own enlightenment.

DENKO-E
Assembly on the Transmission of the Light

DHARMA
The teachings of the Buddha

DHARMADHATU MUDRA
"Gesture of reality"

DHARMAKAYA
The body of the Buddha that is unmanifested, beyond existence or nonexistence

DHARMAS
"Experienced phenomena"

DOAN
The person who sounds the bell which marks the beginning and end of zazen

DOGEN
A Japanese Zen teacher who founded the Soto school after traveling to China and training under Rujing

DOKUSAN
A private meeting between a Zen student and teacher

DUKKHA
A wheel out of kilter. Suffering, dissatisfaction, stress

EIHEIJI
The main Soto Zen monastery, founded by Eihei Dogen in 1244, located in the mountains near Fukui

GASSHO
A position with palms together and fingers pointing upwards in prayer position, expressing greeting, request, thankfulness, reverence, or prayer

HAKUIN
An important Japanese Zen master in the Rinzai lineage, famous for his painting and calligraphy

HARA
The Abdomen
INO
The head of the meditation hall

JOSHU
Zhaozhou in Chinese, Zen master in Seventh Century China, famous for the koan, "mu"

JUKAI
A Zen public ordination ceremony in which a lay student receives Buddhist Precepts

KENSHO
In Zen, "enlightenment," customarily referring to an initial awakening experience

KESA
Refers to the okesa, a monk's robe

KINHIN
Walking meditation

KLISTA
Seventh sense, habit.

KOAN
A story, question, problem or statement, generally not available via rational understanding, but accessible through intuition, considered a test of one's enlightenment

KYOJU
To instruct, to teach

LOTUS
A cross-legged sitting position in which the feet are placed on opposite thighs

MAHAYANA
The form of Buddhism prominent in North Asia, including China, Mongolia, Tibet, Korea, and Japan, called the "Great Vehicle"

MAN PO
Listening to the Dharma

MANJUSHRI
A bodhisattva associated with prajna, wisdom

MARA
The demon that tempts humans in order to distract them from spiritual practice

MENJU
Face-to-face Transmission
MU
"No, not, nothing," in the Chan school, pure human awareness, prior to experience or knowledge

MUDRA
Position of hands and fingers in meditation, literally, "seal."

NEHAN-E
Assembly upon the Parinirvana of Buddha

NIRMANAKAYA
The physical body of a buddha

NIRVANA

"Blown out" as in a candle, referring to the stillness of mind after the fires of desire, aversion, and delusion have been extinguished

PARINIRVANA
Nirvana after death of the body of someone who has attained nirvana during their lifetime

PRANA
Sanskrit for "life force" or vital principle which permeates the universe

PRATITYA SAMUTPADA
"Dependent origination" or "dependent co-arising," meaning that all phenomena exist or come about depending on other phenomena or conditions

PRECEPTS
Behaviors which characterize a buddha. The **Zen Precepts** are not given in the form of commands, but are training guidelines to help one live a life in which one is happy, without worries, and able to meditate well.

ROHATSU
December 8, the commemoration of Buddha's enlightenment

RUJING
Taintong Rujing, gave transmission to Eihei Dogen, called Tendo Nyojo in Japan

SAMADHI
Still mind, total awareness of the present moment, one-pointedness of mind

SAMBOGHA
Enjoyment

SAMBOGHAKAYA
"Subtle body of limitless form," "enjoyment body"

SAMSARA
The cycle of birth and rebirth; the world as commonly experienced

SANCHI
Entering the room of the teacher

SANGE
To regret past harmful actions and resolve to avoid future errors

SANGHA
The community of Buddhist monks, nuns, teachers, and practitioners

SAWAKI
Kodo Sawaki, a Japanese Zen teacher, head of Antai-ji, a temple in Kyoto, famous for his emphasis on "just sitting."

SEIZA
A sitting position where one kneels and sits back onto the heels

SESSHIN
An intensive meditation retreat lasting 1 or more days.

SHAKYAMUNI
Based on the Buddha's clan name of "Shakya", it means, "Sage of the Shakyas"

SHAMATHA
Samatha (Pāli), (Sanskrit: शमथ, śamatha[note 1] is the Buddhist practice (bhavana) of the
calming of the mind (citta) and its 'formations' (sankhara). This is done by practicing singlepointed meditation most commonly through mindfulness of breathing. Samatha is common to all Buddhist traditions.

SHASHU
A mudra used when standing or walking in formal practice situations

SHIKANTAZA
"Just sitting," practiced in the Soto school of Zen

SHUSO
The Head Monk of a practice period

SKANDHAS
Five functions or aspects which constitute a sentient being: matter or form, sensation or feelings, perception, mental formations or impulses, consciousness

SOTO Zen
A Zen sect which emphasizes Shikantaza

SUZUKI ROSHI
Founder of San Francisco Zen Center

TANJO-E

Assembly on Buddha's Birth

TANKA
Often spelled "thangka", it is a Tibetan Buddhist painting used as a teaching tool

TAPAS
Derived from the Sanskrit root word which means "heat" from fire or weather, refers to selfdisciplined efforts to achieve self-realization

TATHAGATA
Sanskrit word indicating one who has transcended birth and death

TOZAN
Famous for the Jewel Mirror Samadhi and five ranks, also known as Dongshan Liangjie

UDUMBARA
The flower which blooms only once in hundreds or thousands of years, which Dogen uses in his explanation of the Flower Sermon given by the Buddha, symbolizing mind to mind transmission between Buddha and Mahakashapa.

VINAYAPITAKA
Monastic rules for monks and nuns, including Buddha's explanations of the reasons for each rule.

VIPASSANA
Insight resulting from the mind state of shamatha

WAY-SEEKING MIND
Way Seeking Mind is the part of oneself that motivates our search.

ZABUTON
A flat cushion which is placed under a zafu and cushions knees and ankles

ZAFU
A round cushion for doing zazen

Zazen
Zen sitting meditation

ZenDO
In Zen, a hall where zazen is practiced

Printed in Great Britain
by Amazon